Understanding Digitalization

A Beginner's Guide To Digital Transformation

TABLE OF CONTENTS

Chapter 1 : The Definition of Digital Transformation   **1**

Chapter 2 : Digitization is Changing the Business World   **11**

Chapter 3 : How Digitalization Impacts Your Daily Life   **29**

Chapter 4 : How to Pay Your Bills Online   **40**

Chapter 5 : Banking Online: Online Payment Systems   **51**

Chapter 6 : Shopping Online   **78**

Chapter 7 : Digital Economy   **96**

Chapter 8 : Why digitization is important for your business   **137**

Chapter 9 : Challenges with Digitization   **156**

Chapter 10 : Case studies   **167**

Chapter 1

The Definition of Digital Transformation

Digital transformation is the procedure of utilizing digital technologies to make new or alter existing business procedures, culture, and client experiences to meet changing business and market necessities. This reconsidering of the digital business age is digital transformation. It rises above conventional jobs, like marketing, sales, and client assistance. Rather, digital transformation starts and finishes with how you consider, and work with, clients. As we move from paper to spreadsheets to smart applications for dealing with our businesses, we get the opportunity to reconsider how we work together, how we draw in our clients with digital technology on our side.

For small businesses starting up, there's no compelling reason to set up your business forms and change them later. You can future-confirmation your association from the word go. Building a twenty-first-century business on sticky notes and handwritten records isn't economical. Thinking, arranging, and building carefully sets you up to be coordinated, adaptable, and prepared to develop.

Numerous organizations are asking whether they are truly doing the correct things.

Before taking a gander at the hows and whats of changing your business, we first need to respond to a fundamental question: How did we get from paper and pencil record-keeping to world-changing organizations based on the back of digital technologies?

What's the difference between digitization, digitalization, and digital transformation?

Digitization is the move from analog to digital

Until quite recently, organizations kept records on paper. Regardless of whether manually written in records or composed into reports, business information was simple. If you needed to assemble or share data, you managed physical documents: papers and binders, Xeroxes, and faxes.

At one point, desktop personal computers (PCs) went standard, and most organizations began changing over those ink-on-paper records to digital computer documents. This is called digitization: changing data from analog to digital.

Finding and sharing data turned out to be a lot simpler once it had been digitized. However, the manner in which organizations utilized their new digital records greatly impersonated the old analog strategies. PC working frameworks were even structured around symbols of record organizers to feel familiar and less scary to new clients. Digital information was exponentially more efficient for organizations than handwritten had been, however, business frameworks and procedures were still planned around regarding how to discover, offer, and use data.

Definition of Digitalization

Digitalization is the conventional term for the digital transformation of society and the economy. It describes the progress from a mechanical age using analog technologies to a period of information and innovativeness utilizing digital technologies and digital business innovation,

Digitalization has various aspects, which are clarified in this article. For instance, the term *digital transformation* describes the progressive progress of existing monetary and social frameworks into the digital age. The term *digital disruption* describes the extreme changes activated by imaginative, advanced plans of action.

Digitalization is using digital data to simplify how you work

The way toward utilizing digitized data to make methods for working less difficult and progressively efficient is called *digitalization*. Digitalization isn't tied in with changing how you work together or making new kinds of organizations. It's about keeping on keeping on, however, quicker and better, since your information is available in a split second and not caught in a file organizer someplace in a dusty file room.

Consider client care, regardless of whether in retail, field operations, or a call focus. Digitalization assistance changes things by making client records effectively and rapidly retrievable using the computer. The fundamental philosophy of client assistance didn't change. However, the way toward handling a request, looking into the significant information, and offering goals, turned out to be considerably more effective when looking through paper records was supplanted by entering a couple of keystrokes on a PC screen or cell phone.

As digital technology developed, individuals began creating thoughts for utilizing business innovation in new ways, and simply doing the old things faster. This is the point at which the possibility of digital transformation started to come to fruition. With new advances, new things—and better approaches for doing them—were possible.

Fields of Digitalization

Since around the year 2000, different digital technologies (mobile phone Internet, human-made reasoning, Internet of Things,[i] and so forth) have been created and have made the change from master application to individuals' regular daily existence.

Similarly, as the development of the steam engine and the spread of power have changed society, so has digitalization changed the economy and society.

Digitalization is technology-driven. Digital innovation is made based on new digital advances: Innovative use cases driven by organizations, as well as new businesses and funding. This prompts a digitalization of various rates. For instance, while the open organization is still regularly just accepting paper archives and working with records, markets are changing much faster. The music and media enterprises were the first to experience the impacts of digitalization. Retail business followed. Essentially, all ventures are currently influenced by the various fields of digitization.

Digitalization decides the eventual fate of the economy and society

What effect will digitalization have for what's to come? Digital transformation is an extreme change in the economy and society that has happened over a time of very nearly 50 years. It started in the mid-1990s with the spread of the Internet and the rise of service providers, for example, AOL and CompuServe. Digitalization was advanced by the expansion in Internet associations toward the end of the 1990s. Digitalization was additionally aided by the fast Internet and mobile information. Later, a significantly faster mobile Internet (5G) joined with technologies of the Internet of Things and artificial intelligence that will make applications such as the expanded utilization of mechanical autonomy, conceivable. Digitalization will change the eventual fate of the economy.

Digitalization changes economy and society

- Digitalization will change the future of the car business through new mobility ideas. From independent heading to existing sharing models and new ideas, for example, the rental of electric bikes, digitalization will permit new models of use later on.

- Digitalization impacts the future of the budgetary business. Technologies, for example, the blockchain empowers new types of corporate financing and support, notwithstanding the applications as often examined in the press, for example, the virtual currency Bitcoin. Today, for instance, organization speculations are made conceivable via so-called ICOs (Initial Coin Offerings) or STOs (Security Token Offerings). These structures are just conceivable through digital technologies, which will keep on spreading.

- Digitalization is changing the fate of customary callings. Eventually, doctors will be helped increasingly more by uses of e-health, particularly in diagnostics.

- Services in the legal sector (today given by legal advisors) will be enhanced or supplanted by digital services from the Legal Tech area.

Someday, digitalization will make new opportunities for schools and instruction, preparing and further training, open organization, and affiliations. It is the duty of industry, associations, and political issues to prepare society for the progressions that can be normal later on from digitalization.

Digitalization and Enterprises

Digitalization has suggestions for enterprises, everything being equal. From one viewpoint, endeavors need to digitize their inward procedures and methods; then again, they need to grow new administrations and advanced plans of action. To a limited extent, this is driven by digital transformation in organizations that have characterized an advanced guide, and by new businesses. In digitalization, the test for organizations is to recognize new client needs because of the developing appropriation of digital services and apps.

New target groups have additionally risen for organizations with the so-called digital natives. To accomplish this, an alternate advertising and deals procedure is frequently required.

Digitalization makes it important for organizations to concentrate their activities on the improvement of digital innovations to be successful in digital change. Ordinary fields of activity are:

- Establish a culture that advances the improvement of digital procedures and techniques and makes it conceivable to create digital services and digital business models.

- Development of digital innovation procedures, for example, an activity plan for the organization's treatment of digitalization.

- Training of representatives to set them up for the difficulties of the digital age and to empower them to participate in digital change.

- Alignment of an organization's marketing and sales to digitalization. Organizations need to manage this question: How would we like to arrive at our clients tomorrow? What job do patterns, for example, content marketing and sales automation, play? How would we manage the perpetually singular needs of our clients?

- Development of digital procedures: Saying farewell to paper records by presenting procedures and techniques in the organization, some of which must be profoundly reconsidered because of digitalization.

- Dealing with information that emerges inside the organization regarding the exercises of an organization or with clients. New assistance and plans of action can be created from the information.

Clients became more educated when the Internet was becoming widespread. New technologies, for example, artificial intelligence and the blockchain, will keep on radically changing plans of action in organizations for the foreseeable future. In this way, digitalization in the organization is a point for top administration.

Innolytics innovation software[ii] helps organizations drive digital change. Inside an organization, distinctive development systems can be established and managed that efficiently advance digitalization.

Digital Transformation adds value to customer interaction

Computerization is changing how business is accomplished, and, sometimes, makes altogether new classes of organizations. With the digital change, organizations are able to get more done, from inner frameworks to client communications, both on the web and face-to-face. They're asking big questions like, can we change our procedures such that it will empower better basic leadership, game-changing efficiencies, or a superior client involvement and more personalization?

Presently, we're firmly settled in the digital age, and organizations of numerous kinds are undertaking sharp, successful methods for utilizing innovation.

Netflix is an incredible model. It began as a mail request administration and upset the physical video rental business. At that point, digital innovations made wide-scale streaming video conceivable. Today, Netflix takes on conventional communication and satellite broadcasting companies and creation studios at the same time by offering a developing library of on-request content at ultracompetitive costs.

Digitization gave Netflix the capacity to not only exclusively stream video content legitimately to clients, but also increased exceptional understanding into review habits and preferences. It utilizes that information to educate everything from the plan of its client experience to the improvement of first-run shows and motion pictures at in-house studios. That is a digital change in real life: exploiting accessible advances to illuminate how a business runs.

A key component of digital change is understanding the capability of your innovation. That doesn't mean asking, "How much faster would we be able to do things a similar way?" It implies asking, "What is our technology able to do, and how might we adjust our business and procedures to take advantage of our technology investments?"

Before Netflix, individuals picked motion pictures to lease by going to stores and going through racks of tapes, searching for something that looked great. Presently, libraries of digital content are served upon close-to-home gadgets, complete with suggestions and surveys dependent on client inclinations.

Streaming subscription-based content directly to individuals' TVs, PCs, and cell phones was a conspicuous disturbance to the physical video rental business. Embracing streaming also led Netflix to investigate what else it could do with the accessible innovation. That led to innovations like a substance proposal framework driven by artificial intelligence (AI).

Adapt your Business to Leverage Digital Transformation

Essentially, digital changes have reshaped how organizations approach client care. The old model was to trust that clients will discover you, whether face-to-face or by calling an 800 number. In any case, the ascent of social media has changed to help a lot; it's changed promoting, marketing, and even deals and client care. Progressive organizations hold onto online life as an opportunity to expand their administration contributions by meeting clients at their foundation of decision.

Making call centers and in-store administration work areas run more efficiently with digital technology is incredible. But, genuine change comes when you take a look at all available advances and think about how adjusting your business to them can give clients a superior encounter. Social media wasn't designed to replace call centers, yet it's become an extra channel (and chance) to offer better client assistance. Adjusting your administration contributions to grasp online life is another genuine case of a digital transformation.

In any case, why stop there? Digital transformation urges organizations to reexamine everything, including customary thoughts of groups and divisions. That doesn't mean tapping your administration reps to run advertising efforts, yet it can mean tearing down dividers between divisions. Your web-based life nearness can include administration and promoting, integrated by an advanced stage that catches client data, makes customized adventures, and channels client inquiries to your service agents.

Goldman Sachs's study shows its presumption of available growth up to the year 2025, being a sort of alert for what's to come. As 80 percent of jobs will include digitalization, there is no reason for the organizations to postpone the digitalization of procedures.

McKinsey's study sees advantages to a business in expanding client engagement and fulfillment, together with the possibility to reduce operational expenses by executing a digital methodology. Clearly, the multifaceted nature of the implementation and the potential cost saving will rely upon the size of the business, yet it's almost guaranteed that if you're pondering this, you're in front of the pack. Furthermore, the primary concern, regardless of the size of your business, is that creating and implementing a digital client care procedure will bring about happier, more satisfied clients, repeat business, referrals, and, obviously, development and benefit. One of the principles of McKinsey's piece was that the more digital the adventure, the higher the fulfillment. Whenever considered, arranged, and managed well, business process digitization projects can have various advantages for an association. For instance, associations can:

- improve business process efficiency, quality, and consistency
- incorporate records with digital frameworks
- improve openness and encourage better information sharing
- improve reaction time and customer administration
- reduce costs
- advance more prominent staff adaptability.

- create a better arrangement for business continuity
- increase customer loyalty

Digital plans of action have brought enormous advantages: operational productivity is expanded, organization development is extended, outside and inside correspondence is synchronized, and new kinds of income streams can show up.

Facebook Inc. is an American organization situated in Menlo Park, California. The organization incorporates the interpersonal organization Facebook, the video and photograph sharing application Instagram, and the messenger application WhatsApp. In 2010, the organization had 2,127 workers, with an income of 1.97 billion, as indicated by Wikipedia. It was established in February 2004 in Cambridge, Massachusetts.

To arrive at acknowledgment for digital transformation, or so-called artificial intelligence (AI) implementation, businesses should sow trust by characterizing the moral standards. As per Christian Kirschniak, partner and head of data and analytics advisory, PwC Europe, the message of the executives ought to be clear: AI needs to replace exercises, not workers.

Chapter 2

Digitization is Changing the Business World

Digitization is significant in our work and the business world, since it adds to its steady change and development. Work doesn't look as it used to 20 or 50 years ago. It turned out to be increasingly flexible and is, by and large, always changing. Here are five ways digitization is changing the business world.

Artificial Intelligence (AI)

There has been extreme discussion on artificial intelligence over the past couple of years.

While a few people (for example, movie makers) have rather dark expectations concerning AI, in actuality, it's an incredible inverse. As indicated by the exploration directed by BCG and MIT Sloan Management Review. Three-quarters of executives trust AI will empower their organizations to move into new organizations. Almost 85 percent trust AI will enable their organizations to attain or continue to have an upper hand.

But AI has just changed the business world to such a degree that organizations use it to automatize work and certain exercises. Among them is performing information investigation, making calculations, or improving correspondence between the organization and customers.

Flexible Work

Because of digitization, we can pick how to function and when to function. With all information and data being put away on digital media and gadgets, we can, without much of a stretch, change it and access it from anyplace. Technological progress and digitization made it conceivable to alter the work calendar to our own needs and way of life. Since numerous organizations utilize innovative devices, an ever-increasing number of organizations depend on freelancers and remote workers, as they can convey their work using the web; sometimes a lot quicker than those working in the workplace.

Innovation

Digitization isn't just about moving information into the electronic form, it also utilizes these devices and finds better approaches for creating them. There are such a large number of new, imaginative arrangements available. Furthermore, they can be applied to practically any part of the business world. Innovation in technology encourages organizations to concoct new thoughts, contact a more extensive crowd, utilize extraordinary devices for sorting out and managing work, and most importantly, make a superior item that fulfills clients needs and upgrades their everyday life.

New Business Models

Digitization made it conceivable to make numerous new plans of action. However, with all the data and tools available on the web, organizations can make plans of action adjusted to their own needs. They can apply new plans to old methodologies, play with assets, and, as a result, build something unique, fresh, and frequently imaginative.

Communication

Communication is one of the most significant parts of our lives. Without legitimate correspondence, a business can't thrive. The absence of the right data leads to mistaken assumptions and clashes.

Fortunately, there are numerous instruments and channels a business can use, both with the workers and customers. There are different stages empowering a smooth trade of data, and even records, reports, for instance, Skype, Slack, online journals, recordings, and even Facebook. Also, there are other tools enabling communication, for example web journals and sites, gatherings, training sessions, or conferences. These are possible thanks to digitization.

7 Examples of How Digital Transformation Impacts Business Performance

Digital transformation includes something beyond refreshing innovation and procedures; it additionally includes income and investors. Numerous organizations are hesitant to put resources into advanced change without knowing whether the venture will pay off. But, when done deliberately, digital transformation can improve stock prices and income over the long-term. The following seven significant organizations show that changes probably won't happen medium-term; however, putting resources into computerized change can have an enormous money-related effect after some time.

DIGITAL TRANSFORMATION TIMEFRAMES AND GROWTH RATES

Company	Years it took for digital transformation	Stock price growth rate
Microsoft	5 YEARS	258%
Hasbro	7 YEARS	203%
Best Buy	7 YEARS	198%
Honeywell	3 YEARS	83%
Nike	2 YEARS	69%
Target	8 YEARS	66%
Home Depot	2 YEARS	59%

BLAKEMORGAN
www.blakemichellemorgan.com

7 Years At Best Buy

Understanding Digitalization

Best Buy Stock Price Performance

Seven years back, many thought Best Buy was dead. Indeed, even individuals inside the organization didn't trust it could make it, due to Amazon. Be that as it may, another CEO and a new digital perspective transformed the gadgets store from a spot to purchase CDs to a digital pioneer in innovation. Rather than simply selling items, the brand plans to improve individuals' lives with technology. To get that going, Best Buy employees endeavored to improve delivery times. It changed its concentration to prompting clients, not simply offering to them. Best Buy workers offer in-home meetings on how clients can best utilize their gadgets, and the Geek Squad will presently fix anything in a client's home for a fixed yearly expense.

Best Buy also progressed from predominately mail advertising to a, for the most part, digital technique. It utilizes information to make client profiles, then gives suggestions and help.

Best Buy's digital change hasn't been without hiccups. However, the outcomes are beginning to appear. Best Buy began 2012 with a stock cost of $23.70. In July 2019, it sold for around $74. Early development was somewhat moderate. Costs have been consistently expanding in the course of the most recent three years while income reduced over that equivalent period. However, it has increased steadily over the most recent three years, bouncing from around $40 billion late 2017 to its current $43 billion.

8 Years at Target

Target re-appropriated its web presence, which they saw as an auxiliary in 2004, to Amazon. However, in 2011, Target recognized what would be inevitable, and chose to reclaim its digital presence from Amazon and focus on it as a principle bit of business. Target has been putting resources into its stores to make another, rebuilt plan that blends the line between internet business and physical stores. More than 400 stores have been renovated and outfitted with innovation over the most recent two years and have presented web-based requesting and in-store pickup and curbside basic food item pickup administrations. Numerous new parts of the store pursue the D2C model by selling select things at pop-ups from well-known brands. Target has also made progress with a reliably captivating web-based social networking app that enables clients to find new items and even get them legitimately through an internet-based life.

Understanding Digitalization

The progressing effort to fabricate an increasingly holistic digital strategy takes into consideration deeper customization. And, it's paying off. Target had been seeing relentless development since its absolute bottom in 2006. Target stocks began 2017 around $73 per share and dropped down to around $53 when the activities sloped in the year, yet as of now, exchange around $88, with development holding steady in that period. In the course of the most recent two years, Target's income has expanded from around $70 billion to $76 billion. And, it's not done at this point: Target intends to redesign another 600 stores by 2020, at an expense of $7 billion.

7 Years at Hasbro

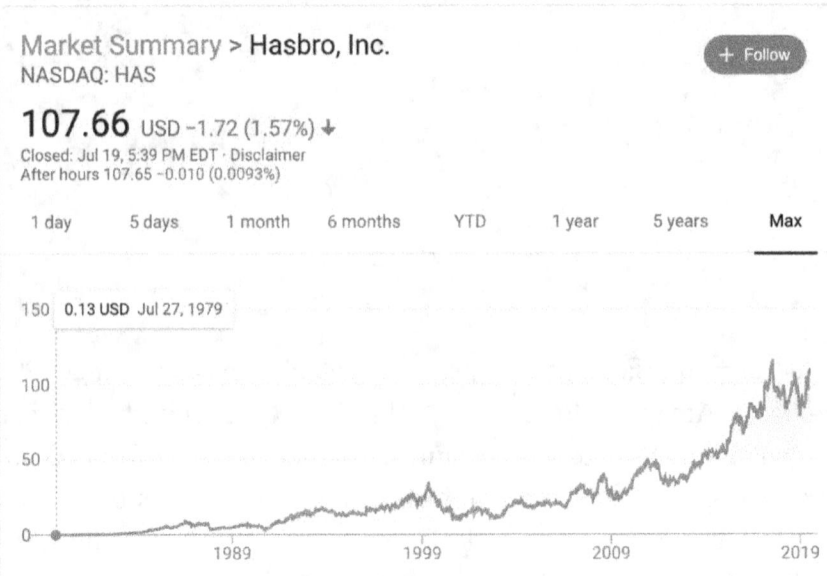

Hasbro's maximum stock value execution

At Hasbro, digital transformation is the play of any child. The toy and game organization made huge interests in its digital and information methodologies that paid off in a major manner. In late 2012, Hasbro understood that as opposed to concentrating on kids, it should showcase their folks, who are the individuals who make the purchases. The organization utilized the information to focus on marketing efforts in different channels, remembering a bigger push for social media. The information helped the organization better understand its clients and prescribe significant toys and games to guardians. Utilizing information additionally helped Hasbro make a frictionless experience as it better added clients and could proactively address their issues.

Hasbro also harnessed the intensity of digital narrating through web-based life and video content. It joined nostalgic brands with groundbreaking channels to interface with clients. Omnichannel showcasing kept the item front of clients' brains for improved associations with the brand.

The change didn't come at a modest cost. Hasbro expanded its advertisement spend by 1100%; however, it had the option to build deals by $1 billion. In 2016, it hit $5 billion in deals. In 2013, Hasbro stock sold for $36; today, it sells for $109. The development was upset by industry changes and unpredictability. However, the attention on digital marketing and information has helped Hasbro face hardship.

2 Years at Home Depot

Home Depot's maximum stock value execution

The Home Depot today has a robust information and IT division to fuel its continuous digital change. In late 2017, the organization said it would contribute more than $11 billion throughout the following three years to improve and consolidate its physical and web-based shopping experiences. It additionally set out to enlist 1,000 IT and client experience experts. Home Depot is moving toward temporary workers and DIYers shopping on the web. The objective is to make a consistent experience across channels and to give the best items and assets to clients. The investment has helped develop the back-end and conveyance channels.

Home Depot has additionally improved its utilization of information to more readily attain clients. By following patterns, it can guarantee the correct items are available without losing cash on excess inventory. It additionally added visual and voice search to its application to give clients more options. Rather than being overpowered by items, clients can, without much of a stretch, locate the correct things and get help realizing how to make home fixes or complete a project.

The blurring between the web and in the store is working. Home Depot's stock has improved from $135 in mid-2017 to $215 today. In a similar time, income has developed from $93.3 billion to almost $110 billion.

5 Years at Microsoft

Microsoft's maximum stock value execution

Microsoft has, for some time, been known for its top items, Windows and Office. Yet, slacking stock prices and expanded challenges from organizations like Apple and Amazon drove the organization to reevaluate its procedure and make a progressively forward-centered cloud business.

At the point when CEO Satya Nadella took over in 2014, the organization started a move towards its cloud organizing frameworks. It moved away from traditional software to a progressively liquid cloud framework for both individual and project use. Rather than avoiding organizations, as it had before, Microsoft changed course to fabricate associations with other programming and innovation organizations. General visibility additionally changed, as Microsoft went from being viewed as an obsolete or stale organization to a groundbreaking cloud arrangement. As it substantiates itself with more plans and development, Microsoft's star keeps on rising.

In mid-2014, directly before Microsoft's change started, stocks were selling at around $38 per share. Today (2019), they're worth around

$136. Over that equivalent period, income expanded from $93.5 billion to $122 billion. Microsoft turned out to be only the third organization to get a $1 trillion market top, prominently before its rival, Google. That achievement wasn't even fathomable only a couple of years prior.

2 Years at Nike

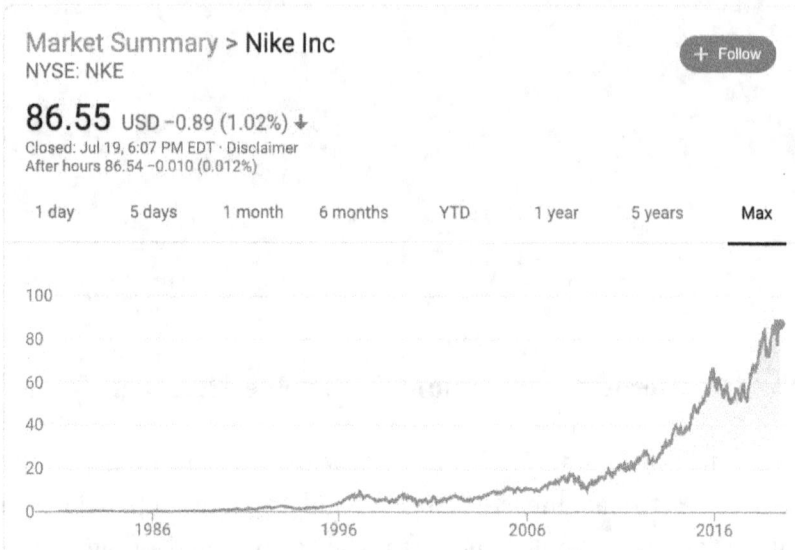

Nike's maximum stock value performance

Although a staple in shoes and athletic clothing, Nike began looking drowsy and outdated a couple of years back. The organization exchanged its attitude and experienced a continuous advanced change to rehash its image and inventory network.

Rather than focusing on brokers, Nike improved its association with clients through participation opportunities, more grounded advanced advertising, and incredible information investigation. Rather than selling through different merchants, Nike began selling more directly to clients, and collaborated with Amazon for a refreshed online business procedure. A start-to-finish center around shopper information better enables Nike to associate with clients and prescribe the correct items. It additionally opened idea stores and improved its web and application experience.

The improved digital focus gives Nike a quicker item advancement cycle, which enables it to get new items to market quickly, react to and set patterns, and control the number of products that are created. A huge piece of Nike's image is the shortage of a portion of its shoes and the coolness factor that makes.

Nike's digital change is continuous as it pushes for imaginative approaches to interface with clients and gets a major advantage over the competition. Toward the start of 2017, its stock value was $52; it's presently (2019) up to almost $88. In that equivalent time, income expanded from $33.5 billion to $39.1 billion.

3 Years at Honeywell

Honeywell's maximum stock value performance

As it plans to assist different organizations with their computerized changes, Honeywell also rolled out significant improvements in itself. A couple of years ago, it streamlined a significant number of its mechanical end showcases by cutting them down from eight to six. The objective was to concentrate on quality over quantity, and utilizing digital solutions. Honeywell utilizes information to decide the best side projects and developments for its organization. Alongside its digital change, Honeywell utilizes information to support its clients. In 2016, Honeywell began its very own interior digital change gathering. It presented new technologies, including more IoT-associated and information-driven gadgets and contributions. As it reexamines mechanical procedure control and offers more innovation answers for its clients, Honeywell also shows its reestablished spotlight on client information and internal solutions. Streamlining inside procedures and digitizing enables the organization to construct quality connections and items.

Since its restored effort started around four years back (2015), Honeywell's stock has expanded from $95 per offer to $174. Its income increased from $40.3 billion to a peak of almost $43 billion in mid-2018, yet it has since dropped back to $38.6 billion. Digital change is a progressing procedure. A commitment to digital transformation and the assets to back it up can transform slacking stocks into industry pioneers. Despite the fact that there are dangers involved, these organizations show that discovering digital arrangements and procedures can lead to long-term monetary profits.

We are a public driven by advanced innovation. Such is its effect that there are nations where residents don't have running water; however, they claim cell phones. Digital marketing has a staggering impact on individuals' associations, work, purchases, and life habits.

Organizations today need to have a firm handle on the most proficient method to use the digital universe to augment their brand awareness and effect. Next, we take a look at nine of the greatest ways that digital marketing has changed, and continues changing, how organizations and brands work.

1) Instant Communication

Communicating with potential clients today can resemble turning a roulette wheel. The roulette ball speaks to the organization's marketing message, which will turn and bounce as the wheel spins before at long last arriving on a space (for example, a client). Web-based life goes about as the wheel itself, and it enables organizations to collaborate with individuals in an open scene, giving a channel to advance items, services, and transparent messages. Yet, there's another player in the game, and organizations need to make sense of how to hop on the famous vessel before it leaves the harbor. According to *The Economist*, a quarter of all downloaded applications are abandoned after a solitary use with just texting evading the pattern.

Facebook Messenger has 900 million worldwide clients, and studies have demonstrated that young people presently invest more energy in informing applications than they do on genuine interpersonal relationships. To take advantage of this blossoming market, keen organizations are presenting techniques for interfacing with and promoting to potential customers through these sorts of uses.

2) Content Overload

Exactly what amount of substance is conveyed using online life and informing applications? The appropriate response is immense, so tremendous that it has been given the term *content stun*. Like clockwork, 3.3 million individuals make a Facebook post, and 29 million messages are sent using WhatsApp. That implies that advertisers have their work removed if they will get their message and brand seen by the individuals utilizing these applications.

Rolex is an incredible case of a classic brand that is utilizing imagination to get its promoting message across to clients and potential clients. As a brand with 112 years of history behind it, this could present issues in keeping the brand new. However, Rolex overcomes this by making high-quality and appealing item images that have a curated feel and feature the classic nature and unwavering quality of their product. Utilizing in-vogue and moderate pictures in its photography, recordings, and writing, it shouts class to clients by featuring its quality items and timeless tagline.

3) Droves of Data

Current innovation enables advertisers to store a huge amount of information about their clients. Organizations need to know how, where, and when to utilize that information. Ideal approaches to achieve this are:

- Knowing which measurements are generally critical to organization achievement. The key is to be quite certain about what the business results are and incorporate that with how the information is used and how it impacts the business.

- Knowing which client channels are going to pay off. The variety of advances and channels means that a brand needs to concentrate on the ones that their clients want. Likes and remarks may appear to be significant, yet the main thing is a commitment that forms a connection between a client and a brand.

- Having workers with the scientific skills to process information. All the information on the planet is pointless without the ability in-house to recognize how to manage it. Bits of knowledge from information is what can drive a business and assist it with understanding the behavior and pain points of a buyer.

- Creating content that is customized and client-centered. The huge amount of information on the internet makes it difficult for any brand to have a genuine effect. The key is knowing who the intended interest group is and making content that catches their eye and urges them to lock in.

4) Demands Transparency

In the present digital world, clients need to think about the organizations they cooperate with and buy from. To create dedication, brands should be simple and show their character and the organization's ethos on the web. This is especially pertinent with regards to nourishment items, with purchasers needing to know precisely what's in the things they eat.

In a study by Label Insight, just 12% of shoppers trust organizations with regards to packaging, and search for data on the item somewhere else, although 67% believe it's dependent upon the brand to furnish them with this data.

For those organizations that do discuss things transparently with clients, the prize is loyalty, with 94% of shoppers professing to stay with an organization that offers transparency, and 73% would pay more for an item that offers it.

This requirement for transparency in nourishment packaging stretches out to numerous parts of the business from how it gets its representatives and what it offers back to society and networks. Digital leaders will get this and guarantee that their clients are educated with important data, be it good, bad, or ugly.

5) Fosters Intimacy

Organizations can become familiar with a colossal amount of information about potential clients, dependent on the information they can assemble. Savvy organizations are utilizing this information to make very close-to-home advertising messages, and the younger age is eating it up.

Social goings-on and the impression of others is a driving spark among twenty- to thirty-year-olds. This makes personalization an amazing asset, as 85% of clients are bound to purchase an item if the message is personalized and supported by social media. One organization that exceeds expectations around there is EasyJet.

To celebrate 20 years in business, the organization analyzed their information to perceive what bits of knowledge could be accumulated from clients, and discovered inspiring pieces of data about their clients' adventures. The outcome was an email battle utilizing dynamic duplicate, pictures, and connections to recount to every client's story from their first trip to ones later on, including some fascinating facts about their movement behavior and suggestions for future trips.

What came about was open paces of over 100% over a normal EasyJet pamphlet, with 25% higher navigate rates. Via web-based networking media, individuals responded within minutes with an overwhelmingly positive reaction, with a span of 685,000 individuals and over 1.1 million impressions. Also, over all business sectors, 7.5% of clients who got the email made a booking in the following 30 days.

6) A New Breed of Influencers

Internet-based life and video outlets like YouTube have empowered average individuals to become amazingly powerful.

Presently, ordinary people with no credentials other than droves of adherents via web-based networking media can impact an organization just by embracing a specific item. Take Swedish online entertainer PewDiePie, with more than 47 million followers. Even those with below 100,000 devotees may have more impact and higher commitment rates than traditional VIPs.

Mindful of these new influencers, brands have taken to procuring influencers to convince and connect with clients. Take Coca-Cola, for instance, which has moved from a dependence on influencer item arrangements to contracting influencers as hosts and starting their own YouTube channel, Coke TV.

This has made a connection between the brand and the crowd a long way past the standard item position. Young is somewhat exhausted of publicizing," expressed Philip Hartmann, head of content at Coca-Cola Germany.

7) Playing Catch-Up

Digital technology changes at a staggeringly quick pace. These progressions require representatives across divisions to be nimble, work cooperatively, and, in particular, keep up with the latest advancements so they can adjust and utilize these progressions to the organization's benefit.

Training representatives is an extraordinary method to achieve this. By up-skilling a workforce in the most recent and most significant advancements, procedures, and strategies, representatives can be proactive and see how their image can utilize these progressions to further their potential benefit.

Take IBM, for instance. Intensely mindful of the changing scene, they presented a digital selling test case program that changed their conventional deals group into digital sellers. The pilot demonstrated so successfully that it has now been turned out on a worldwide scale to change the selling abilities of its staff, drive income, and improve its mindshare and status across online systems.

Fundamentally, to make advanced progress, organizations should know about the pace of progress and put resources into learning and improvement activities that guarantee their workforce are on the cutting edge of digital marketing and selling strategies.

8) Encourage Innovation

This new scene has constrained brands to be creative, utilizing better approaches to connect and draw in with their clients. Despite disrupters, numerous areas have been imaginative and take steps that empower them to contend. Take the financial sector for models, money-related foundations require better approaches to draw in and impact clients.

For some, teaming up with the best in class is viewed as the ideal approach to achieving this. Through advancement focuses, significant players in the business—for example, HSBC and JP Morgan—are grasping the new universe of digital to serve their clients better. Opening an advancement lab in the Asia Pacific demonstrated a flash of brilliance for HSBC, which created cutting-edge digital and mobile banking services. The point is for this lab to reinforce the bank's worldwide program of development so they can use global reach and network.

9) Made Brands More Human

Because of its popularity and impact, web-based social networking showcasing ought to be upfront on any organization's advertising methodology, as clients need to trust and comprehend the organization they are purchasing from.

One of the best instances of an organization that has got this idea down to craftsmanship is Apple. Key advertising guarantees that brand awareness rules preeminent among its clients, and it's viable to the point that Apple has a huge number of individuals supporting their items before they are even on the market!

They accomplish this by utilizing live occasions, bringing about crowds of clients that vibe like they are a piece of the brand's adventure, and all things considered, when Apple launches another item, they have a committed and attentive audience.

Chapter 3

How Digitalization Impacts Your Daily Life

Since the early 2000s, our lives have been gradually taken over by innovation. Pause for a minute to check it out. What number of screens do you see? Did you incorporate the one you're reading this on?

Our Wi-Fi-empowered devices have changed how we work, play, and even bring up our kids. The present workplaces would be unrecognizable to laborers of the past thanks to the expansion of messages, video conferencing, tablets, PCs, and other advancements. In the meantime, more of our own time is increasingly impacted by our devices (OK, cell phones. So, have we arrived at the top of innovation? Barely.

The novelty of constant online associations and immediate correspondence may have started to wear us ragged. Our tech-subordinate ways of life are as of now causing major changes in both the professional and private circles. The change might be unavoidable, unless we lose Wi-Fi.

Our Digitized Professional Lives

A 2013 Pew Research study discovered that "94% of jobholders are Internet clients." This incorporates full-time, low-maintenance, and independent specialists in innovation organizations, large partnerships, and private companies who work in urban communities, suburbia, rural America, and anywhere in the middle.

For the greater part of the last century, communicating professionally meant writing letters, sending faxes, or going through hours on the telephone. Not any longer. Email is presently an essential method for correspondence in the advanced work environment. We are communicating more, faster, and above anyone's previous imagination. And, bosses have been receiving the rewards. A significant report referred to by British paper the *Telegraph* found that the incorporation of innovation into the working environment has prompted an "84% expansion in profitability every hour for office laborers since the 1970s." The significant influencers? Email, business programming, and, indeed, even mobile phones.

Technology Gets Personal

We don't leave technology in the working environment. Our private lives may be significantly more tech-empowered than our work lives. During the 1980s and 1990s, our TVs were frequently the stature of our home innovation. A few people had clunky personal computers, a Nintendo for the children, and possibly a phone in their vehicle (recall those?).

Data from the Census Bureau discloses that 15% of homes had a PC in 1989; by 2011, that number moved to 75%. Presently we have workstations, cell phones, tablets, Apple watches, GPS-empowered vehicles, and more tech coming each day. Forget unplugging after the 6 o'clock whistle blows; we plug in.

Going tech may trigger an existential emergency for a few (that sound you hear is Albert Camus turning over in his grave). Our technology causes us to learn, date, eat, socialize, and considerably more.

The main time we don't utilize technology is when we are sleeping; until further notice…

A New Generation of Digital Natives

Anybody conceived before the coming of innovation in their everyday lives is viewed as a "digital immigrant." Older folks concocted our tech-empowered society when they were young, yet the ages conceived in this thousand years are the first true "digital natives. While the "digital rehab" programs more established ages have started utilizing to push back against the all-expending digital saturation are picking up footing, these projects may bode well to younger ages as getting up from the lounge chair to change the channel on the TV. The genie is out of the bottle, and innovation is said to have even changed how more youthful generations see reality.

We're expecting they see reality as that thing happening just into the great beyond of their laptop, tablet, or cell phone screen (as long as somebody is tweeting about it). Despite the fact that it's not difficult to ridicule the cutting edge's digital obsession, it will before long be difficult to disregard it. The digital natives are poised to dwarf digital immigrants very soon.

The Bottom Line

Technology is presently so incorporated in our lives that abandoning it can cause extreme anxiety for a few. It's not hard to perceive the reason why.

Both our professional and individual lives are currently technology-dependent. While older folks are retaliating with unplugged withdrawals, many Americans can't picture their lives without tech. They probably won't have anything to stress over. The future supports these digital natives.

As indicated by a Pew January 2014 overview, Internet use by older Americans has expanded around 73 percent since 1995. Americans live probably some segment of their lives on the web. While some may claim the Internet is chaining us to our devices, making us avoid human contact and sometimes even daylight, the Internet has also given us better approaches to convey, learn, and investigate the world at large.

Sharing and the New Media

Anybody can impart data with the click of a mouse thanks to the Internet. Digital media are easy to share and simple to make. A substance maker needs a digital camera and an Internet association to transfer his next motion picture. YouTube permitted excellence master Michelle Phan to dispatch a delighted realm from her lounge. Indeed, even as customary media extended their venture into purchasers' homes through the Internet, new stages developed online, like Netflix, Amazon Prime, and HBO Go. As indicated by Forbes, Netflix has outpaced link organizations in watchers.

You've Got Mail

An Internet connection gives a channel to extending human associations around the globe. Keeping in contact with your child in school or your family on another mainland is a simple task with email. The minimal effort of conveying information on the Internet has also changed telephonic and television administration. Next time you have to communicate with a companion or schedule a prospective employee meet-up, make it up close and personal. Services like Skype and Facetime make distance irrelevant. Friends around the world can participate in discussions from the comfort of their own homes.

Social Networks

Social media have made it simpler to interface with others and extend your group of friends, who need not rely upon face-to-face meetings in your regular daily existence. You can presently contact anybody with an Internet association; you can watch their lives unfold in real-time, and record the occasions in yours. Vacation photographs go up on Facebook and Instagram, and dates are booked on Tinder. Interpersonal organizations empower clients to share more pieces of their lives than at any time in recent memory.

Beyond the Bank

Digital money makes it simpler for anybody to encourage money-related exchanges. Regardless of whether you use PayPal or Venmo, the Internet has brought down the expense of working together. If you need some assistance beginning a business or financing a good thought, crowdfunding sites like Indiegogo can assist anybody with a convincing story to begin. Thanks to the Internet, new financial tools are changing how we consider cash and working together.

The Sharing Economy

Sharing economies make how individuals live their lives increasingly proficient. Customary organizations are facing the innovations that peer-to-peer communication and information-sharing bring to the economy. Because of Uber,[iii] for instance, vehicles that generally would travel half-empty are profiting. Airbnb[iv] enables an individual to make an additional salary from an empty room. The Internet enables people to grow their projects into new markets, improving the state of their financial balances simultaneously.

Education

One of the most significant things the Internet has brought us is access to education. Students need not rely upon customary study halls to learn. Students supplement homeroom learning with Skype mentors or a survey session with an online video instructional exercise. The Internet has democratized education. For instance, the *New York Times* announced that Google has been taking a shot at approaches to carrying the Internet to remote zones of Africa, giving small towns better approaches for accessing data and working and communicating over long separations with companions, partners, and family.

New frontiers of health: mHealth and self-administration of sickness

The principle commitments addressed by the digitization of health and the experience of illness is adequately evolving. The most talked-about issues are self-administration, understanding strengthening, and the board's responsibility using digital stages. Specifically, the commitment of Benjamin Marant entitled "Advanced advances and the reconfiguration of health experiences and practices" featured, in a fascinating examination on the usage of mobile health (mHealth) to empower self-service of HIV patients, that there is a specific level of strengthening that leads expanded individual duty regarding wellbeing. One's checking can cultivate a more noteworthy familiarity with their health, yet is joined by a reductionist understanding of health. In the commitment exhibited, the patients in the trial are wondering about the right method to utilize the mobile application and don't surrender to the assessment of the specialist. This may lead to a reflection on the best way to coordinate specialist and new e-health technologies.

The key issue for the advancement of e-health is the rise of new methods for correspondence, empowering health experts, organizations, patients, and the overall population to remain connected. The commitment entitled "Self-service and measured self: how diabetes applications cultivate checking" by Barbara Morsello and Veronica Moretti concentrated on the investigation of the application for the service of type 1 diabetes, emphasizing how the services accessible with these applications, for example, the insulin number cruncher, may lead a mistaken or unseemly portion proposal or the intensity of affecting different patients especially youthful, beginning with blood-following practices. These applications are frequently planned with levels of gamification.

A part of the field of e-health identifies with virtual health. Virtual health refers to the probability of another body outperforming its physical skills and points of confinement to increase new capabilities as a superhuman advancing in a virtual world. We presume that computerized consideration developments encourage the following of human services practices, and the capability of the mHealth stage for self-management in ordinary practices and authoritative schedules should not be neglected.

Emotional Quantification: happiness as a measure of progress

An extremely interesting presentation entitled "Joy as a Measure of Progress: Digital instruments of arrangement making" by Anat Noa Fanti investigated the outcomes and discoveries raised from the examination of satisfaction and well-being indicators utilized in different worldwide settings. The creator's point of view began from the historical and social investigation of the idea of happiness, to arrive at the resolution that feelings are estimated as any element of present-day life, for example, profitability, the nation's political life, health, etc. Happiness in this new total structure, away from abstract feeling, suffers a social move: it gets something reasonable, intelligible, as far as circumstances and logical results, and consequently quantifiable. Subsequently, the joy pace of a nation can be estimated; it can be developed through making the conditions through indicators that governments deem reliable. Happiness and its ordering make the various nations practically identical here and there and, in this way, puts them on a scale from least to generally upbeat. Satisfaction is no longer inside the nation and residents, yet it becomes something outside to equitably measure. The entrancing purpose of this talk concerns the dangers that this pointer of satisfaction and prosperity could turn into another approach to direct oneself and the subjectivity of residents, taking with it the latent imposition of new standards and desirable models.

Digital Subjects in Online Spaces

Technology is, in this way, not neutral in light of the fact that it is an outflow of the individual. The technologies are anthropomorphic and recreate our activity, which is constantly founded on values. The social world that we produce is the reflection of virtual situations we possess, and we structure with our mediation. Along these lines, we can support that online is the connection between our being and our doing, or, rather, it is the outflow of our being as doing. The contribution of Patrick Keilty entitled "Digital Subjects in the Graphical Interface of Pornography" planned precisely to get a handle on the element of qualities in the development of digital subjects of graphical interfaces of online erotic entertainment sites. The improvement of graphical interfaces is founded on the maximization of pleasure, through a cliché vision of the client and his needs. This generalization manages the development of the online conditions that depend on clients, from the point of view of expenses and advantages. The creator utilizes the instance of pornographic sites to feature the need to build up the online space as a continuation of the physical space of relations without losing human measurement.

Powerful Problems Drive Powerful Dreams

By 2050, there will be 9 billion people on the planet to feed, dress, transport, utilize, instruct, and engage.

Billions are focused on the development and are driven by the world economy. As we seek unlimited development, our boundless utilization uses up everything else on Earth. We are warming the atmosphere, overspending our monetary assets, requiring more freshwater than we have, increasing income inequality, diminishing other species, and triggering shockwaves whenever we can't cope with a problem.

Billions of individuals are at the base of the economy. The white-collar class is declining. Youth underemployment is an epidemic in numerous nations. The gauge for billions is to stay stuck for their entire lives.

Leaders need new alternatives as much as every other person. There is space to dream about an increasingly effective world alongside new technology.

Will a New Digital Window Display a New Future?

This new choice began in 2007 with big questions: Can we imagine a reality where tech assists everybody succeed and prosper? Can that world be planned and fabricated now, without sitting tight for "the future" to show up?

The Expandiverse developed through long stretches of private and classified tech and IP (Intellectual Property) improvement.

Our reality is full of screens. We keep them in our hands, purses, and pockets, by our beds while we rest, and surround ourselves with screens on our work areas and ledges. Our TV sets are transforming into intuitive screens as we put them on the web, so they show everything for nothing.

Imagine a scenario where every one of our screens, all over the place, was a two-way organized framework that transforms the Earth into an advanced live with everybody in it. Imagine a scenario in which that arranged framework brought everybody the world's best services, assets, and information dependent on what we do as an ordinary piece of regular day-to-day existence.

Billions of us. Together. All prevailing as much as we choose. Constantly.

We should dream a bit. We should dream about innovation we could work, about a world we could appreciate.

Turn On a You-Centered Digital World

If your future gadgets were continuous, your power over the entirety of your gadgets, and the nonstop digital world they could open for you, could expand exponentially.

You switch between numerous screens. At the point when you leave your old screen, it stores where and what your identity is. Your new screen remembers you, turns on, and recovers where and what your identity is. It is genuinely programmed.

Understanding Digitalization

A wide range of things are before you. They could be applications or programming, digital content (books, TV, motion pictures, music, recordings, and that's only the tip of the iceberg), games, or live video from around the world. They could even be different gadgets and sources you control remotely.

Your advanced life will consistently be on, constantly open, forever yours. You'll live in your "Common Planetary Life Spaces."

Indeed, it's genuine to the point that your "mutual spaces" move with you over your screens, and become one of your realities. It's the digital world you pick, where you can live—continuously prepared for you to use in the manner you need.

Innovation is going to move a lot quicker and join with entertainment until life is excitement and diversion is life.

In the expandiverse, you will get used to your picked digital truths being shown and handled without exertion. Numerous screens, various characters, and different, changed video, sound, and music feeds will essentially show up, and you will show up in them.

In your digital life, you can stroll through a wonderful new daybreak. Or then again, your very own activity movie sequel, with you as both one of the executives and one of the stars.

You can make any or the entirety of your digital worlds' outputs visible to anybody you wish. What is still called "publishing" or "broadcasting" can be practiced in a huge number of ways with a large number of results.

You are the publisher. You are the telecaster. You are the digital reality maker.

You pick your private or open crowds. They can utilize your creation, or show up in it. Or on the other hand, you choose to be the crowd and show up inside your digital world.

Quite a bit of your life is as of now you-focused. Next, your digital life will let you become the individual (and individuals) you've constantly longed to be. Since restorative science can't stretch out our lifetimes to hundreds and thousands of years, the expandiverse offers different characters. Okay, consider appreciating various lives in parallel? This won't be for everybody, except for the individuals who can't get enough out of one short life; it could be their pass to more lives and a superior method to be alive.

Your digital life is a reality. Any place you truly are.

For billions of individuals the whole way across the Earth, yesterday's reality isn't succeeding. Too many are stuck, educated, aware, capable, and connected, yet secured to a constrained future rather than allowed to take off.

Something different Expandiverse innovation offers is called Active Knowledge. Might we be able to outperform the physical world's points of confinement on our futures? Imagine a scenario where the best information, instruments, assets, and chances to succeed could be delivered as a major aspect of what we do each day, as we utilize our screens. Everybody could get ready to proceed just as the best on the planet.

At that point, with an all-inclusive interface, everybody could run their whole Expandiverse from all over the place. It won't make any difference whether you're in Silicon Valley or a little town in Africa.

Truly, you will be a worldwide individual who associates all over the place. Also, indeed, the entire world and its best information and assets will be a neighborhood to you, readily available, under your influence.

Everyone could rise to the top.

Would it be a good idea for us to start the adventure into a digital existence where everybody could decide to be their best, where significance could be ordinary?

Understanding Digitalization

As our digital world develops, gadgets should expand until your gadgets can serve you completely. This won't occur without any forethought. In any case, it's an ideal opportunity to begin understanding that it will occur.

Not at all like any age before have we realized how to design and build our dreams. Grow your brain and extend your future.

Chapter 4

How to Pay Your Bills Online

Taking care of your bills online makes it a lot simpler procedure. It can save time, set aside your cash, and make your life a lot easier. You have a few choices with regards to covering your bills on the web. In actuality, you will most likely utilize a mix of the various choices to pay most of your bills on the web.

Separate Your Bills into Three Piles

First, gather the entirety of your bills and separate them into three piles. The primary heap ought to be the bills that are a similar sum every month, for example, credit installments or the linked bill. The subsequent pile should be monthly charges that change from month to month, for example, the power bill or your Visa bill. The third heap ought to incorporate bills that you don't pay all the time.

Set Up Automatic Drafts

You should begin by setting up automatic drafts to cover every one of the bills that are a set sum every month. Most organizations offer the choice of automatic draft. It is ideal to do an automatic draft just with charges that are reliably the same every month. You can either set it up through the utility or credit organization, or you can plan it with your bank. A few organizations charge a preparing expense for automatic installments, so you might be in an ideal situation setting it up yourself.

- Subscriptions to things like streaming services or links normally fit into this classification.

- Rent or home loan installments are other choices.
- Insurance installments will likewise fit in this classification.

Utilize Your Bank's Payment Service

To set up a recurring installment with your financial record, you have to visit the Bill Pay segment of your internet banking page. You will set up a profile for the bill that you need to pay on the web. This profile will incorporate your account number, the location that the installment will be sent to, and the organization's name. At that point, choose to set up a repetitive installment. You will set a date for the draft to be pulled. To make the procedure simpler for you, you can also set this up on your computer software, with the goal that it automatically updates for you also.

- Some banks may restrain the number of online installments you can make without an expense.
- Smaller banks might not have the same services as bigger banks.

Decide the Bills You Will Pay Online Each Month

Next, consider the bills that you pay month to month in which the amount due changes. Paying this every month will assist you with tracking your costs better and keep you from overdrawing your account. First, go into your bill pay record and set up a profile to take care of the bill. At that point, when the opportunity arrives to make an installment, you will choose the one-time installment alternative, click on the profile of the charge you are paying, and enter the sum. Make certain to record the exchange number the bank gives you as a receipt.

Plan for Your Annual Bills

The irregular bills that you get might be dealt with in a different way. It would incorporate things, for example, your tag and registration renewal for your vehicle, or it could be a quarterly bill. These bills you can either set up a profile for on your bank or visit the organization's site or cover the bill online. By and large, there isn't a handling expense to take care of the bill on the web if it is an irregular bill.

Tips:

1. When you take care of your bills online, you should plan the installment to be pulled a couple of days before the bill is due. It will enable the installment to be on schedule if there is a bank holiday or weekend. Furthermore, it gives you an opportunity to make remedies if the installment didn't occur for reasons unknown.

2. You can set up updates in your planning programming that will tell you that your installment ought to have been drafted from your account. It will assist you in keeping a running balance of your financial records and reduce the probability of overspending. You can save money on banking charges if you prevent yourself from overdrawing your account.

3. Although it is tempting to disregard your bills once you have set up programmed installments, it is critical to check occasionally to ensure that everything is being paid on schedule. It will keep you from allowing a mix-up to happen. You should open your bills every month to ensure the installment has not gone up or that the due date hasn't changed.

4. Another motivation to check your bills every month is that the bills may go up. For instance, a streaming service may raise its rates. If you are checking your bills every month, you can decide whether you need to keep on utilizing the service or search for better rates. You should look for protection all the time.

The Most Effective Method to Organize Your Bill-Paying Process

For some of you, bill-paying may be one of your least-loved chores. But it's a significant one. Without a framework for taking care of bills, payments can be late or missed, bringing about late charges and higher fees. Late payments can also destroy your credit.

You can avoid this by composing your bill-paying procedure and keeping it sorted out. You'll require a computer, a lot of plastic or cardboard drawers, a junk can, a paper shredder, a red pen, note pad, highlighter, 10" x 13" envelopes, and stamps.

Create a Bill-Paying Station

Taking care of bills will be easier if you have a particular bill-paying station you can sit at. It doesn't need to be a huge space: a little table toward the side of your kitchen, a rack in your home office, or just a basket to hold your bill-paying instruments and supplies.

Organize Your Paper Bills

Most organizations have a paperless charging choice nowadays; however, if despite everything you get some paper bills, you can use these means to process them.

Open them when they show up.

Utilizing a red pen, make a note of the due date and the sum owed on the front of every envelope. Give close consideration to due dates, since they're not generally the exact same date every month. At the point when you read through your bill, note any charges that you question with the goal that you'll have the option to effectively catch up on these issues later.

Recycle any envelope stuffers that don't contain any personal data. Shred whatever has a name, address, phone number, or account number on it. On the off chance that you don't own a shredder, you can find one that you can use at an office supply store for a small fee.

Lastly, store your unpaid bills in the front of your plastic or cardboard cabinet framework.

Organize Your Electronic Bills and Statements

Utilize a different email address for electronic bills, bank statements, investment statements, etc. This will guarantee that you don't overlook an electronic bill amidst the different messages you get.

View your online bills and statements when you get the messages. Confirm that you are in concurrence with the entirety of the charges and the sum due. If you discover an inconsistency, print out the record, note the charge, and put the paper in your plastic or cardboard cabinet framework alongside your unpaid paper bills. If you don't own a printer, make a note of the issue in your notepad and put the journal in a similar cabinet. You'll manage any errors later in this procedure.

Next, forward each email to your email address and change the title to incorporate the entity owed, due date, and the sum due—for instance, GA Gas, 6-28-2019, $78.

Make an email organizer on your PC or distributed storage for every month and year. You can name it "Online Bills—[Month] [Year]." After you've checked each online bill and sent it to yourself, store it in the month-to-month organizer you made.

Timetable: a Weekly Time to Pay Your Bills

Take 30 minutes every week to take care of your bills. Put this time on your schedule the same as you would some other arrangement. This is also a great time to audit your online financial balance for accuracy.

Go to your bill-paying station and pull the paper bills from your to-be-paid cabinet. Sign on to your PC and open the current month's to-be-paid envelope. If you noted any questions or discrepancies, make calls to these institutions first.

If you can't get through to anybody, add this assignment to your plan for the following day. Make a note of your record number, the customer care telephone number, and your particular question.

Pay Your Bills

Think about online bill payments. There are two regular kinds of online bill pay choices.

- Online pay offered by your bank;
- Online pay offered by your specialist co-ops (telephone organization, contract organization, and so on).

While it might take you more time at first to set up online payment installments, you'll save time during each consequent month by paying your bills on the web. In both online bill-paying situations, you'll be given a confirmation number as a major aspect of the exchange. Make a note of this data either on the charge itself or keep a rundown of the month-to-month exchanges in your notepad.

If you're not paying your bills on the web, write out your check, record the exchange in your check register, utilize the return envelope that comes with most bills, and stamp the envelope. Make certain to factor mail time into your procedure.

While you won't have a confirmation number, you should now make a note of the exchange on the charge itself or your rundown of the month-to-month payments. Make a point to also include your check number.

File the Paper Copies of Your Bill

Make a 10" x 13" envelope for every month. When you're finished paying the bills, place the paper duplicates in the proper month's envelope alongside your master list of transactions (that will likewise remember data for the bills you get electronically). If any of these bills are tax deductible, make a duplicate and record it with your yearly tax reports.

How to Manage Your Bills Better With Quicken Bill Pay

Quicken Bill Pay is an online bill pay service that fills in as an extra with Quicken individual fund programming. The extra is free for Quicken clients who have Premier plans or better. Otherwise, the service currently costs $9.95 every month.

Advantages of Using Quicken Bill Pay

Valuable services and features on Quicken Bill Pay include:

- The software is good with several payees.
- Email notices get sent to you when bills show up.
- Payments made online at the Quicken Bill Pay webpage automatically get moved into Quicken desktop software.
- Repeating charge payments take into consideration both variable and fixed month-to-month sums.
- Details for each bill can be seen inside the product.
- Bills can be paid from inside Quicken software or directly from the Quicken Bill Pay site.
- Pay up to 10 records from numerous banks.
- Quicken Bill Pay offers an on-time payment assurance and will pay late charges up to $50 if a bill is paid late.

Utilizing the Bill Pay Service

Quicken Bill Pay has a basic setup procedure, and bills can be paid utilizing any US financial record. The site stores payee details—for example, account numbers and other data—for you, so you need to enter sums and schedule the installments. You can process installments promptly as you enter them, or schedule payments for future dates. You can also set your recurring payments to process each month.

Setting Up Quicken Bill Pay

Setting up Quicken Bill Pay requires individual data that you'll need to assemble in advance. Required data incorporates financial records details and government-managed savings numbers. To begin, visit the Quicken Bill Pay site. From that point, existing Quicken clients can click "as of now have Quicken?" and new clients can click "get Quicken now." Complete the registration form, and you'll be prepared to set up your records. This procedure can also be begun through Quicken software.

Adding Your List of Payees

A payee in Quicken Bill Pay implies any organization, service, or individual you'll be paying through the service. A payee can be a service organization, for instance, or a bank for your home loan credit, or your landlord.

When setting up payees, you will give essential data about the individual or the business you'll be paying, for example, payment address and account number. Quicken saves this data in your payee list so you can make payments to that payee again later on without having to reenter the data.

Set up payees by following these steps:

1. Click "Instruments" in the menu and select "Online Payee List."
2. Click "New."
3. Enter the name of the new payee.
4. Enter the location of the new payee.
5. Enter the account number for the payee.
6. Enter the telephone number for the payee.
7. Click "OK."

After this starting step, the site will add your new payee to your payee list. From that point on, you need to choose the payee from your list.

Best Online Bill Paying Software and Services

The Internet has made efficient online bill payment workable for the general population. You can utilize an online bill pay service to set up a protected online account that lets you take care of every one of your bills from one spot.

Online bill pay saves time and effort, and automating your online payments encourages you to keep away from late payments in spite of your busy timetable. Numerous banks offer some bill-paying elements through their sites. Read on for more data about the best online bill pay administrations.

Paytrust[v]

Use Paytrust, and you will most likely never get another paper bill again. This online bill pay service can make payments to any organization or individual in the US. The organization holds pictures of bills and installment data for a long time, and you can get a CD that contains a record of your yearly bill installment information.

Quicken Bill Pay

Quicken Bill Pay fills in as an online bill pay service that you can use with Quicken individual account programming, yet you don't need to purchase Quicken to utilize the service.

Despite the fact that it's not as highlight-rich as Paytrust, Quicken Bill Pay offers a large number of similar features. Stimulate Bill Pay additionally offers a free trial.

MyCheckFree[vi]

MyCheckFree, from the financial assistance company Fiserv, is outstanding amongst other free online bill pay service available.

MyCheckFree lets you take care of bills online from several organizations. Scout the pooch, the administration's mascot, "brings" bills for you. It might appear to be somewhat silly. However, the cost of MyCheckFree (it's free) makes the pooch very middle of the road.

Yodlee[vii]

Online individual finance software Yodlee enables you to set up online bill pay through various banks or credit cards. Yodlee doesn't charge for the administration; however, check with banks or credit cards you need to use as funding sources to find out whether they will charge an expense.

In addition, Yodlee's Bill Pay Account Accelerator makes it simple to switch funding sources for installments.

Mint Bills

Mint is a free online individual fund service from Intuit that encourages you to deal with your accounts and records on the web.

Mint takes care of bills using Mint Tabs, and offers a free help that lets you total every one of your bills in a single spot and pay them with a financial balance. You'll pay a charge to pay with a credit or check card.

Mint Bills offers the standard features, for example, the capacity to set up updates for bill due dates and cautions for low assets in real money accounts.

Mint Bills additionally offers versatile applications for iOS, Amazon, and Android gadgets.

Banks, Brokerages, Credit Cards, and Online Financial Apps

Numerous banks, brokerages, and credit cards offer free online services, including charge payment, through their sites. Notwithstanding, these internet banking locales may not give every one of the features that a devoted online bill pays service offers. Think about the purpose behind utilizing web banks and their services to discover whether they can address your issues.

Money-related organizations that offer bill pay benefits, for the most part, let you plan payments ahead of time, and if you have a charge card that grants money back for purchases that you take care of consistently, utilizing this kind of online bill pay can be particularly valuable.

Chapter 5

Banking Online: Online Payment Systems

There's no denying that with regard to accepting and receiving payments, PayPal is the prevailing hero. Indeed, it's the accepted online payment answer for online clients, specialists, and entrepreneurs.

While individuals will, in general, love PayPal for an assortment of reasons, innovation has opened the entryway for various contenders to challenge PayPal by offering less expensive rates, quicker exchanges, and upgraded security. Here are some of those other options.

1. Due

Due became famous through its creative time-following and invoicing devices, which are particularly helpful for freelancers and small business owners. As of late, Due has enabled clients to begin accepting secure online payments for only a 2.7 percent exchange rate. Due additionally acknowledges worldwide payments, which ordinarily happen inside two business days, just as an advanced wallet to send or get cash to anybody on the planet immediately with practically zero expense. It even has an e-bank where you can store your money on the web.

2. Stripe

Stripe has interested clients for the most recent few years with its incredible and adaptable API. This implies you can tailor the stage to meet your particular needs, regardless of whether you're running a membership organization or a commercial center. Stripe coordinates with several different applications, so regardless of whether you're an expert coder or not, you can get ready for action rapidly. The absence of arrangement, month-to-month, or hidden expenses is a special reward.

3. Dwolla[viii]

Dwolla has similar features to PayPal with regard to moving assets, yet on account of its API, it concentrates more on bank moves, or Automated Clearing House (ACH) payments, so clients can make a customized payment arrangement where payments are received inside a day. The best part is that exchanges are free.

4. Apple Pay

If you're a trader, consider accepting Apple Pay. Exchanges are quicker and progressively secure, since Apple Pay utilizes contact ID affirmation. A client can utilize their unique finger impression to pay for their takeout pizza. Apple Pay is still moderately youthful; however, don't be shocked if the service will adjust to help more seasoned machines. Also, word on the street is that Apple is taking a shot at a P2P payment framework inside iMessage.

5. Payoneer[ix]

Payoneer is one of the most established worldwide payment processing services. It is accessible to more than 200 nations and acknowledges 150 unique monetary standards. Accepting payments is free, and it incorporates an adaptable API that develops with your business. Like PayPal, you can get a plastic credit card if you aren't 100 percent digital.

6. 2Checkout

2Checkout is another contender in the payment arena that enables clients to acknowledge charge cards, platinum cards, and PayPal comprehensively. It's accessible in 87 distinct languages, offers advanced fraud protection, incorporates several web-based shopping baskets, and enables you to easily charge clients with repeating charges.

7. Amazon Payments

If you need to give clients genuine feelings of serenity, acknowledge installments through Amazon. At whatever point they make a buy on your site, they consequently experience Amazon's checkout. This means they'll utilize their Amazon credentials, which makes the checkout procedure progressively helpful and reliable.

8. Square[x]

Square changed the game when it presented its magnetic stripe reader, enabling entrepreneurs to swipe charge cards anyplace for a 2.75 percent exchange expense per swipe. But, you can also send electronic invoices and get paid, through the Square Cash App.

9. Skrill

Skrill has features like withdrawals and stores, low exchange charges, restrictive offers, the capacity to acknowledge from 40 monetary standards, and having the option to send instant messages directly from your record. If you refer a friend, the organization will put 10 percent of the expenses they create from paying or sending cash into your Skrill for a whole year.

10. Venmo

Despite the fact that PayPal obtained Venmo, the essential standards are diverse between the two. PayPal is utilized for making simple transactions for either personal or professional purposes. Venmo is utilized by people who think about themselves as social spenders. As such, it resembles a mixture of PayPal and an interpersonal organization like Facebook, since transactions are shared on an online channel. So at whatever point a companion repays a companion, it's shared freely.

11. Google Wallet

Also known as Google Checkout, Google Wallet is an online payment service that enables clients to send sheltered, basic, and quick cash moves from their program, cell phone, or Gmail account. You can store credit cards, check cards, debit cards, and even gift vouchers to your account.

12. WePay

WePay prides itself on its first-class client assistance and fraud protection. Clients can make their purchases without leaving the site, on account of a virtual terminal. WePay also offers to Know Your Customer assortment and can be utilized for invoicing, occasion ticketing, and advertising mechanization.

13. Intuit GoPayment[xi]

Intuit is essential for an entrepreneur. Other than having the option to acknowledge payments both on the web and face-to-face with the portable GoPayment charge card processor, Intuit can help you with payroll and calculating taxes. The most encouraging highlights are the low monthly price of $19.95, which charges a 1.6 percent charge for credit card swipes, rather than the standard 2.40 percent rate.

14. Authorize.net

You can't forget about Authorize.net. It's been preparing installments since 1996! It's additionally the Internet's most generally utilized payment portal and has been the beneficiary of the Achievement in

Customer Excellence (ACE) grant from 2008 to 2016. Despite the fact that the organization has been around for a long time, it remains current with patterns, such as having the option to acknowledge Apple Pay. No big surprise the organization is so generally respected!

Today, online organizations have more payment choices than at any time in recent memory. Every stage accompanies its very own points of interest and fallbacks, and it's dependent upon you to discover which is best for your business. Which installment stages have streamlined your business exchanges previously? Which stages do you plan on attempting?

Five Advantages of Online Banking

Most banks offer web-based banking, and you can cover your tabs, move cash, and access a record of your financial transactions, all from your internet browser. Banking from the solace of your couch makes all that you do with your accounts somewhat simpler. An ever-increasing number of banks enable you to store checks by essentially snapping a photo of the check with your telephone. You can get to your financial data anyplace that you approach the Internet, such as on your PC or cell phone.

You may choose to change your accounts to an online-only bank later on. These banks offer the greater part of similar focal points online as a customary bank. However, online-only banks have no physical branches. While this may appear to be an issue, online-only banks offer a couple of advantages that may make it worth the trade-off.

Take care of Your Bills Online

You can utilize your bank's online webpage to cover your bills and shield yourself from having your check get lost in the mail. Most banks will have a segment wherein you set up payees. You should fill out the data once, and afterward, you can essentially pick that profile each time you take care of a bill on the web.

If your bank doesn't take care of bills on the web, you may think about paying through the organization's site. Be cautious, since some of these organizations may charge an expense. A few will charge an expense for plastic, but not if you set up an immediate charge.

If you get to your bank's site on your cell phone, the bank's application normally enables you to store checks with only a depiction of the archive. This means you can deal with the entirety of your banking while never heading off to the bank. Be that as it may, keep your eyes open for any expenses related to online bill pay.

View your Transactions

Web-based banking enables you to get to your account history and exchanges from anyplace. This is the speediest method to check whether an exchange has cleared your account. You can also discover the amount of exchange after you have lost your receipt. It also enables you to get some answers concerning unauthorized transactions all the more rapidly, helping you settle any issues immediately.

A few banks will show you pending charges. These are exchanges that you made that day. If you spot something you didn't approve, you can contact your bank and the merchant to turn around the charges. The sooner you get an issue this way, the more rapidly you can resolve it. Pending exchanges may not be for the accurate measure of the purchase. For instance, on the off chance that you leave a tip, this won't appear on the pending exchange, so remember that as you balance your record.

Move Money Between Accounts

Web-based banking also enables you to move cash between accounts substantially more rapidly, and keep an eye on your accessible assets before going through cash. It is more helpful than utilizing the robotized telephone support and can spare you an excursion to the bank.

At the point when you apply or set up your web-based banking, be certain that the entirety of the accounts you have at the bank are recorded.

You additionally have the alternative of moving cash between various banks on the web. This won't occur as fast, since the cash still needs to go between budgetary foundations. However, it is significantly more advantageous than running to the bank.

Contingent upon the kind of account, your bank may constrain the number of online transfers and may hit you with an expense if you go over.

You can go on the web and move cash to various investment accounts to put something aside for different objectives, for example, a rainy day account or an upfront installment for another home.

Mobile Banking

Most banks will have a portable application that enables you to exploit the internet, putting money on your telephone. This makes web-based banking progressively helpful and enables you to rapidly determine the status of your account when you are out shopping, move assets over in case you're short, or verify whether a merchant has double-charged you. But, you should be certain you are getting to this data on a protected system and avoid utilizing open Wi-Fi while finishing these transfers. Portable finance makes internet banking significantly simpler.

Synchronizing With Your Money Applications

Numerous cash applications will naturally match up with your web-based financial data. This makes sticking to your spending plan a lot simpler. Applications will frequently work both on your PC and your cell phone, so you can keep up-to-date while you are in a hurry. It is additionally simpler to curb your spending for your financial limit if you are utilizing one of these applications.

It's getting substantially less normal to get paper statements, yet it is important to balance your account at your bank every month to keep you from overdrawing. If your bank is small, it may not offer the matching-up work. However, you can update your records every day by signing on and entering your records physically.

Perhaps the best use is that you can synchronize investing so that if you and your partner shop independently, you don't overspend without knowing it.

Online-Only Banks

The entirety of the above advantages apply to both customary accounts with an online presence and online-only banks.

One of the most tempting highlights of online-only banks is the higher premium you'll get on your reserve funds and other money-related items, for example, CDs. These banks have significantly less overhead to pay, and they give the reserve funds to their clients. Different advantages include:

- Lower service and support charges than you would pay with a conventional bank

- No bank offices, which implies you may save more since you can't stroll into a branch to get money

- Good or even extraordinary client assistance, because online banks commit a great deal of their money-related assets to information variety and continuous customer-facing process improvements

- Doing your part to safeguard assets by going with online banking, because conventional banks utilize much more assets, for example, paper and power, among others, contrasted with online-only banks

Secure Yourself Online

It is essential to be cautious when banking on the web, as you don't need your security to be broken. It is essential to clear the cookies after each financial session if you are on an open PC.

Furthermore, ensure that your secret password is sufficiently long enough to keep it from being hacked, and never give your online account data to somebody who isn't an authorized signer. You should make a point to secure your secret phrase, particularly if you have roommates. Also, check your credit report consistently. These means ought to protect you from data fraud.

Online Banking

Online banking gives you the capacity to work your finances remotely. You don't need to go to a bank, send anybody checks, or trust that days for transactions will occur.

Maybe the most empowering component for web-based banking is the headway of web innovation. The speed of the web has gone up in the most recent decade. As indicated by the measurements, the normal web speed in the US has gone up by 500%, from 3.07 Mbps in 2007 to 18.7 Mbps in 2017. In December 1995, just about 0.4% of the total populace at that point, or around 16M individuals, were utilizing the web. In December 2017, conversely, 54% of the total population or 4.7B individuals were utilizing the web.

Also, speed and access, another factor from the purchaser's perspective, has been the increase of mobility. The utilization of mobile internet is on the ascent now, and in the US has gone up from 62% in 2002 to 95% in 2018. Moreover, tablets and PCs have expanded the capacity of an individual to get to the web in a hurry.

From a bank's viewpoint, the advancements in internet protocols have expanded the security of exchanges. Individuals are additionally utilizing applications to do exchanges, prompting an expansion in the volume of transactions.

Online Banking Fraud

Banks reveal to us that banking on the web is protected. But, as indicated by Financial Fraud Action (FFA) in the UK, in the principal half of 2014, internet banking extortion in Britain came to £29.3 million ($47.6 million). This was a 71% expansion from the previous year. Moreover, this was just *detected* bank fraud.

The report creators recommended that in spite of increasingly secure sign-in forms, Internet fraudsters were picking up. As such, British banks and their clients seem, by all accounts, to be getting increasingly defenseless against online fraud.

Banks are constantly attempting to be one step in front of digital crooks. In September 2014, Barclays Bank presented a biometric reader. This reader utilizes fingerprint confirmation innovation. This implies clients can get to their online financial balances with no requirement for codes or passwords.

Online Banking—Bank with Caution

Pretty much every bank today offers web-based banking. There are such huge numbers of non-banking, money-related organizations, like insurance, that are facilitating online banking transactions.

However, the appearance of remote access has also prompted an expansion in fraud. Phishing has been consistent stress for banks. There are different manners by which fraudsters get sensitive data, like passwords and personal identification numbers (PINs). Barclays UK created a commercial a couple of months back to notify individuals how simple it is to get their pin.

Also, fraudsters send messages with interface controls, or they can make whole sites to imitate the bank's site. The phishing attempts may be significantly progressively inconspicuous, such as popups on your bank's real site. This is accomplished by either altering the site or sending an infection to your PC.

Understanding Online Banking

With online banking, customers aren't required to visit a bank office to finish the majority of their fundamental financial exchanges. They can do the entirety of this in their very own comfort, anyplace they need to; at home, at work, or in a hurry.

Online banking requires a PC or other gadget, a web association, and a bank or credit card. To get to the service, customers need to register for their bank's internet banking service. To register, they have to make a secret key. When that is done, they can utilize the support to do all their banking.

Banking transactions offered online fluctuate by the establishment. Most banks commonly offer fundamental services, for example, moves and bill payments. A few banks also enable clients to open up new accounts and apply for credit through web-based financial gateways. Different capacities may incorporate requesting checks, putting stop payments on checks, or changing an address.

Checks would now be able to be kept online through a mobile application. The client enters the sum before snapping a picture of the front and back of the check.

Online banking doesn't allow the acquisition of traveler's checks, bank drafts, certain wire moves, or the finishing of certain credit applications, like home loans. These transactions still need to occur up close and personal with a bank delegate.

What would we be able to do as customers?

Here are a couple of things that you have to do as a purchaser.

1. Never give your password to anyone.
2. Have an antivirus program on your PC. Never turn a firewall off.
3. If you are uncertain about anything, don't utilize it! Stroll into a bank and request help.

4. Always log out from the account after using; abstain from utilizing open PCs for signing in to check your financial balance.

5. Never click on links that appear to be unrealistic.

6. If offered, utilize a two-factor validation for extra safety. Numerous banks today issue either a physical or a virtual gadget for this.

So, internet banking is the most advantageous approach to perform transactions. If you are in France, Selectra.info has a far-reaching article on web-based banking, looking at the different web-based financial choices you have as a buyer. You can analyze the banks and see what works for you.

Online Banking Services

Skipping an outing to the branch implies you can lead business whenever from (nearly) anyplace. Yet, what can you truly achieve? A great deal.

To bank on the web, you'll have to utilize your PC or an application on your cell phone. The beginning can be dubious, in case you're not happy with innovation. However, everything gets simpler once you're set up.

Open accounts: You can open checking, reserve funds, and different accounts on the web without the need to print or sign anything. Before, you needed to sit with an individual broker during business hours and battle off various attempts from them to sell you something. With electronic signature ability, the whole procedure may take under ten minutes.

Pay bills: Instead of writing checks to take care of bills, your bank can print and mail a check for you. It's additionally conceivable to move cash to your payee electronically, regardless of whether the sum you owe changes each month.

Move reserves: Need to move cash from your financial records to your investment account? What about placing additional money into a certificate of deposit (CD) or opening a new CD? You don't have to visit a branch to complete those things. You can even connect ledgers at various banks and zap cash to and fro.

Apply for credit: Loans are a paperwork-concentrated procedure. Be that as it may, they don't need to be. Type in your data, which will speed the way toward checking your credit, and your bank will get back to you with an answer. A few moneylenders work altogether on the web, and they can settle on nearly immediate loaning choices.

Get great rates: Online banks are known for focused rates. In principle, you ought to have the option to win more in online investment accounts and pay lower financing costs on credits. It's constantly a smart thought to search around and contrast web-based financial rates with conventional rates, yet you'll quite often improve on the web. Some physical banks offer online-only alternatives. To utilize those records, you'll need to surrender your paper proclamations (which you may lean toward, in any case) and the capacity to save money with a teller.

Store checks: When someone pays you with a check, there are a few different ways to store it. The quickest and least demanding choice is to utilize remote check store: Snap a photograph of the check and submit it to your bank for installment. There's no compelling reason to visit a branch or mail the check in. For more subtleties, figure out how to store checks with your cell phone.

Remain educated: Notwithstanding physically checking your account on the web, you can utilize old-fashioned instant messages to deal with your account, check adjustments, and that's only the tip of the iceberg. Once in a while, it feels like an excess of work to open an application and sign in to discover the amount you have accessible. Discover precisely what sorts of services are available and how you profit by messaging with your bank.

Understanding Digitalization

View history: Need to check whether that check cleared, or what amount your boss paid you? It's easy to see transactions on the web and download historical statements.

Avoid charges: Online financial administrations usually cost less than conventional physical accounts while offering aggressive rates. You have a decent possibility of finding free financial records and keeping away from monthly support charges with an online bank.

Advantages and disadvantages of Online Banking

There are various advantages to web-based banking, and it's worth having the choice to bank on the web. However, conventional banks and credit associations have their place.

In-person benefits: Banks accomplish something other than hold cash and mix it around. They can give public accountant services, security store boxes, and official checks in a moment. You probably won't require those services regularly; however, when you do, it's ordinarily during a significant occasion. Assess whether it bodes well to keep a nearby account open.

Innovation issues: If you're not happy with innovation, web-based banking might be more inconvenience than it's worth. Also, glitches occur, and if your PC (or the bank's PC) isn't working, at that point, there's very little you can do. For complex circumstances, like pesky client assistance issues or talks about various kinds of credit, it may be ideal to have an up close and personal discussion.

No money? There's additionally the issue of getting money. Online-only banks ordinarily give a charge card that you can use to pull back money, and they may even have a place with systems with free ATMs. In any case, for huge stores or withdrawals, a branch is usually best.

Security

The entirety of this may sound great, yet, is your cash safe?

Online banking is commonly viewed as more secure than conventional banking. Having your compensation legitimately stored in your financial balance eliminates the risk of someone taking your check from the mail. Also, it's not possible for anyone to duplicate your account data from checks that you send to billers when bank PCs send that data to and fro safely. If fraud or errors happen, government law frequently insures you, as long as you act rapidly.

Remaining safe is generally simple. Keep your PC and gadgets modern. Specifically, guarantee that the working framework, antivirus programming, and firewall are kept current. Utilize hard-to-figure passwords, and never record them. Never react to messages, telephone calls, or instant messages that request that you give sensitive account (or individual) data.

Certainly, tricks happen on the web. For whatever length of time that you send cash to someone that you're 100 percent certain you know, you ought to have the option to evade the greater part of them. Remember that the least secure activities are giving cash or data to another person.

The greatest advantage of an online bank is the expense. While numerous conventional banks charge monthly expenses if you don't meet certain criteria, that isn't the standard in online banks. Many assist you with staying away from expenses inside and out, including those horrible overdraft charges that can increase quickly. Besides, they additionally offer portable stages where you can look into your balances and exchanges, take care of bills, store checks, move assets, and more.

Concerning the cons, one to consider is the way that you can't store money. Café servers, valet parkers, and other laborers generally prefer their tips in cash. There's additionally no in-person client assistance, so if you need assistance making sense of something, you'll be on the telephone or web visiting with a client assistance agent. All that stated, read on to discover more about the best online banks and see which fits you best.

Best Online Banks of 2019

- Ally Bank: Best Overall
- Capital One: Best for People in Big Cities
- Charles Schwab Bank: Best for Frequent Travelers
- Simple: Best for Budgeting
- Axos Bank: Best Old-School Option
- Discover Bank: Best for Rewards Checking
- Chime: Best for College Students
- TIAA Bank: Best for High Balance Checking Accounts

Best Overall: Ally Bank

The best online bank in general is Ally. Ally Bank unites low charges, high loan costs, and extraordinary client assistance. Partner offers checking, reserve funds, currency market, CD, and IRA accounts, in addition to the bigger Ally family which incorporates credit cards, automobile loans, home mortgages, and investments. It is a full-service individual fund organization that can deal with a lot of your banking and other cash needs.

Ally's financial records offer premiums, have no monthly expenses, incorporates free utilization of any Allpoint ATM, and gives you to $10 per statement period in charge refunds from other banks' ATMs in the United States.

Web and mobile banking incorporate free moves to accounts at different banks, versatile check stores, quick and free moves to loved ones with Zelle, and every minute of every day telephone client care. Taking a gander at the site; you can see the holdup time to converse with a human. As of this writing (and numerous different visits to the Ally site), that hold time is 0 minutes.

At Ally Bank, you can do pretty much everything except store money. There are a few charges for less regular exercises, like returned goods, overdrafts, and medium-term charge pay, yet the vast majority won't pay any expenses for an ordinary month in any Ally account.

Best for Those in Big Cities: Capital One

Capital One Bank is an extremely close second place, and may be the online bank for you on the off chance that you live in a huge city like Los Angeles, New York, or Dallas, all home to Capital One branches and bistros. These areas do give you a couple of choices for in-person banking. However, the essential Capital One financial experience is still online.

Capital One is a full-service money organization with financial balances, charge cards, automobile loans, and a speculation stage. In contrast to most online banks, Capital One likewise offers business ledgers, seemingly the best web-based checking and reserve funds choices for a private company.

The 360 Checking account is a top-of-the-line financial records across the country, and also, its 360 Savings offers extraordinary loan costs and low expenses. Capital One offers free Capital One and Allpoint ATMs, yet no repayment on other bank ATMs. It makes up for that with adaptable overdraft alternatives, however, including a choice to dismiss overdrafts and charge no expenses if you accidentally swipe your card when you don't have the money to pay for it.

Best for Frequent Travelers: Charles Schwab Bank

Charles Schwab is one of the greatest and best rebate business firms in the nation, yet its financial balances are another convincing motivation to look to Schwab for your cash needs. The main drawback of Schwab's astounding Investor Checking account is that you need to initially open a Schwab money market fund first.

Schwab's Investor Checking is an extraordinary account for any individual who much of the time ventures. This account offers

Understanding Digitalization

unlimited repayments of other bank ATM charges, including universal ATM expenses, which implies you can utilize it to get expense-free money anywhere in the world.

It also has each element you would anticipate from an online bank, including moves to accounts at different banks, remote check stores, and an industry-leading mobile application. Loan fees are not astounding. However, they are higher than the normal physical bank. By and large, it's an extraordinary account.

Best for Budgeting: Simple

Simple is a more current bank, a startup established in 2009 and acquired by BBVA in 2014. This bank doesn't look like numerous different banks, and that is something worth being thankful for. It offers an incredible web-based checking item, implicit planning, and no charges.

Simple doesn't charge any expenses for anything whatsoever outside of utilizing your plastic outside of the United States, and that is a go-through charge charged by Visa, not Simple itself. So you can say that Simple is a no-expense bank and a stand-out bank in such a manner.

The genuine intensity of Simple is its web-based planning devices. Simple encourages you to deal with your cash by utilizing the web tools that enable you to plan and put something aside for objectives.

Best Old-School Option: Axos Bank[xii]

The web may not be a physical spot you can go to. However, that didn't prevent Axos Bank from planting a banner and guaranteeing its online status route in 1999. Bank of Internet is the most seasoned online-only bank in the United States.

Axos Bank offers financial accounts with up to 1.25% premium, low-charge advances, and even online business banking. Axos Bank has aggressive rates for investment funds and CDs, too, alongside low charges in all cases.

Axos Bank was a pioneer in running a bank without a physical branch. They began the model of low overhead and giving the investment funds to clients. If you need to bank on the web, Axos Bank will treat you right. Make a point to peruse the terms for any new account, as some have the least balance needed to stay away from a monthly charge.

Best for Rewards Checking: Discover Bank

The vast majority know Discover as a charge card organization, yet it likewise runs a well-known online bank. The bank offers a scope of web-based financial items, including checking, investment funds, CDs, currency markets, and IRAs. Be that as it may, the most energizing account at Discover will be Discover Cashback Checking.

This account has no monthly expenses and offers 1% money back on up to $3,000 every month in check card purchases. That is up to $360 every year in rewards. Remember the one major drawback of this account: the check card is Discover marked and isn't as broadly acknowledged as Visa and Mastercard.

Besides that, there is little to gripe about with this account. It is low-charge, incorporates access to 60,000 expense-free ATMs, and even gives you your checks and check reorders for nothing.

Best for College Students: Chime

If you need an online financial balance that makes everything simple, consider Chime. Chime charges no expenses, and digital natives will feel comfortable with its simple-to-utilize, versatile application. Chime offers a financial account. However, it is an extraordinary account.

One fun component is the capacity to gain admittance to your direct deposited check early. While most finance runs on Friday, the payment data is likely conveyed to your bank a couple of days prior. Chime offers access to your money as long as two days quicker than different banks.

Chime also offers no overdraft expenses, no monthly charges, no base parity prerequisites, and no remote exchange expenses. They don't offer ATM repayments, however, they give you free access to 30,000+ MoneyPass ATMs and won't charge you any expenses itself for utilizing an out-of-network ATM.

Best for High Balance Checking Accounts: TIAA Bank

Florida-based TIAA Bank offers a Yield Pledge Checking account that is one of a kind among financial balances. It vows to constantly offer loan costs in the main 5 percent of all financial records in the bank and thrift industry.

The account requires a $5,000 opening balance. While the account doesn't charge a monthly expense, you need to keep that $5,000 balance to meet all requirements for unlimited ATM repayments. The account offers a first-year assurance of 1.01% APY on balances up to $250,000, and tiered loan costs extend from 0.25% to 065% after the principal year, depending on your balance.

This account doesn't charge many expenses. However, there are a couple for unusual actions, including a substitution platinum card. By and large, it is a low-expense, high-interest account that you might need to consider on the off chance that you keep $5,000+ in your account consistently.

Online banking, or E-banking, offers you a fast and advantageous approach to deal with your cash. Though it changes from bank to bank, there are commonly not many sorts of exchanges or other service activities that are impossible online with a set-up account. Because this kind of procedure manages individuals' cash, safety efforts must be powerful, and most banks have layers of security at work.

1) Account Management

Online banking frameworks enable you to sign in through their site and view your account data. There might be a few passwords or sign-in codes you need to use to access your account. You can check your present balance and balance history, start moves among account, and view account activity. You can also arrange a check and view check pictures with this kind of banking service.

2) Deposits and Payments

The direct store is a kind of banking that enables you to give a steering number so cash can be moved into your account. It is also possible to set up automatic payments so you can take care of bills and have the sum pulled electronically from your account. This sort of banking is a simple method to take care of repeating bills like utility payments and insurance premiums.

3) Debit Card

Debit cards work like credit cards, aside from that they pull cash from your ledger, and are one of the most widely recognized sorts of online banking transactions. At the point when you utilize a debit card, data about the purchase is placed into PC frameworks and afterward transmitted online to you, where the exchange is prepared inside your account.

4) E-statement

E-statements, or electronic explanations, are your ordinary bank proclamation made accessible on the web. As indicated by GSA Federal Credit Union, e-statement is protected by electronic shields and are in reality, less inclined to get by character cheats than a paper explanation sent through the mail. Numerous banks and credit associations prescribe this sort of web-based banking for security reasons.

How to Set Up Online Banking

Ask your bank if they offer online banking, and they can send you the details you need to set it up.

At the point when you set it up on another or existing ledger, your bank will send you login details by post or email. A few banks let you set it up when you apply.

At the point when you sign in, you will, as a rule, need to enter:

- Your username or client number
- A password
- Other security data

Keep this information safe. Here is the way to keep your banking secure and how to set a strong password.

Utilizing Card Readers

A few banks give their clients card perusers, which are plastic devices that you use to sign in to your account.

1. Insert your card into the reader
2. Enter your PIN
3. The card reader shows a code that you can enter online to sign in

A few banks offer a key card instead, which works similarly. However, you don't have to embed your card into it.

How To Use Online Banking

You can sign in to your account to check:

- Your balance

Understanding Digitalization

- Recent transactions
- Full monthly statements for your account

If you find a suspicious transaction—for example, cash is paid out for something you didn't purchase—contact your bank at the earliest opportunity.

Most banks let you decide to get to your statements online as opposed to sending you a monthly paper statements.

Some offer incentives, like a higher financing cost or no monthly charge, if you go paperless.

You can move cash online from your financial balance to:

- A companion or relative's financial balance
- Another account in your name
- An organization's account if you have to take care of a bill

To send a payment:

1. Sign in to your web-based account through your bank's application

2. Select the send and payment choice

3. Enter the sort code, account number, and name of the payee account

4. Pick a reference (ordinarily your name or what the installments are for; if you are covering a bill, a few organizations determine the reference they need you to utilize)

5. Check that the details are right

6. Send the payment, and the assets should leave your account right away

A few banks have additional security measures if you have to send cash to an account you have not paid previously. They may require you to:

- Enter your password once more

- Generate a password utilizing a card peruser, key card, or their application
- Log in utilizing a PC as opposed to a mobile application

Despite the developing popularity of online banking, not every person is convinced that it's beneficial to change from conventional banking at a branch. To advise you regarding the advantages, here are the main reasons why you ought to consider checking out web-based banking.

1. Comfort

The clearest advantage of web-based banking is comfort. Unlike neighborhood offices are that open during specific hours of the day, online banking is available nonstop at whatever point you need it.

There's additionally no compelling reason to sit around driving to your neighborhood office or remaining in line to wait to address a bank employee. At the point when you bank on the web, you can spare heaps of time by doing everything without anyone else—regardless of whether you have as few as five minutes to sign in to your bank's site and take care of a bill.

2. Direct Control Over Your Transactions

You get the opportunity to be your very own bank employee when you bank on the web. For whatever length of time you understand the essentials of utilizing the web to finish simple tasks, you ought to have the option to explore your bank's site pretty easily to make your exchanges.

Also, utilizing online banking for essential transactions, like bill payments and moves, you can exploit a few extra services you used to have to do by visiting your neighborhood office. For instance, opening another account, changing your account type, or applying for expansion on your credit card limit should all be possible on the web.

3. Access to Everything All in One Place

When you visit your bank face-to-face and get a teller to do all your banking for you, you never get the opportunity to see a lot of anything aside from what shows up on your receipt. With web-based banking, you get the chance to see precisely where your cash is at this moment, where it previously went, and where it needs to go.

Online banks ordinarily give you access to:

- The current balance of each financial account you have at that specific bank (for example, checking and investment funds)
- The current balance of each charge account you have at that specific bank (for example, Visa or MasterCard)
- Account transaction history
- Pending transactions
- All charge payees and bill payment history

4. Lower Banking Fees and Higher Interest Rates

Decreased overhead expenses related to the virtual idea of internet banking enable banks to offer their clients greater motivators for banking on the web with them. For instance, a few banks charge no expenses for online investment accounts that keep up a base balance.

Numerous online-only investment accounts likewise offer higher loan costs, in contrast with banks that keep up nearby offices. You might need to look at Bankrate's[xiii] list of investment account rates in case you're keen on exploiting higher loan fees with your internet banking.

5. Paperless Statements

There's no need to wait for your bank to mail your statement via the post office when you opt for paperless e-statements. There's also no compelling reason to make room in your home for physical stockpiling of the entirety of your transactions accessible to you on the web. Numerous banks enable you to see e-statements for periods dating quite a while back in time with only a couple clicks of your mouse. And, to sweeten the deal even further—irrelevant to banking—you'll be doing the planet a favor by cutting paper utilization.

6. Automated Account Alerts

At the point when you opt to get e-statements rather than paper statements, your bank will, in all probability, set up an alarm to advise you by email when your e-statement is prepared to see. You can likewise set up alarms for a few different exercises.

You ought to have the option to set an alert to inform you regarding your account balance, to reveal to you whether an account has gone above or below a certain amount, to tell you when your account has been overdrawn, and to advise you when you've nearly arrived at your credit limit. You can even go past the nuts and bolts by setting up alarms for when a bill installment has been prepared, when a check has cleared, when future-dated exchanges are coming up, and more.

7. Advanced Security

Banks pay attention to security and utilize a scope of security instruments to guard your data. Your data is encrypted to ensure it as it goes over the web, which you can check by searching for the https:// and the safe latch image in the URL address bar of your internet browser.

If you become the casualty of direct money-related loss because of unapproved account action, you should be completely repaid if you advise your bank about it. As per the FDIC, you have as long as 60 days to tell your bank of unapproved action before you risk unlimited customer liability.

Online shopping is getting progressively well-known for a variety of reasons.

There are unquestionably outside variables, for example, expanding gas costs, trouble in getting to customary stores, and the bother regularly connected with shopping centers and other customary stores to add to the increased interest in online shopping.

Buyers can get full data about the item, with its reviews being given by current clients. If one needs to purchase an item, he/she is never again restricted to asking friends and family, in light of the fact that there are numerous item surveys on the web.

Online shopping sites contain a wide assortment of products, both high caliber and low quality.

Web-based shopping is the way toward inquiring about and obtaining items or administrations over the Internet. Some online stores started a new business in 1992, and web-based retailing assumed control over a critical fragment of the retail showcase during the main decade of the twenty-first century, as responsibility for PCs expanded and retailers started to offer their items over the Internet.

Electronic commerce is utilized for both business-to-business (B2B) and business-to-consumer (B2C) exchanges. Purchasing items from an online shop, e-shop, e-store, web shop, web store, online store, or virtual store is like obtaining items from a catalogue. Online stores depict items available to be purchased with content, photographs, and mixed media records. The client chooses things to be purchased on a request structure known as a shopping basket or cart, and pays with a charge card or some electronic payment. The items are then delivered to the client's location, or with advanced media items, for example, music, programming, digital books, or motion pictures, might be downloaded onto the client's PC.

Online shopping has a few points of interest over shopping in retail locations, including the capacity to effectively think about costs from a scope of merchants, access to a wide choice of products, and the comfort of not heading to a physical store. Online sellers have refined delivering techniques. However, online shopping can't replace the experience of shopping in a retail location or the excitement of heading off to a shopping center or market.

Chapter 6

Shopping Online

History

Beginnings

The idea of online shopping predates the World Wide Web. An innovation for continuous exchange preparing from a residential TV, in light of Videotext, was first shown in 1979 by Michael Aldrich, who planned and introduced frameworks in the UK, including the first Tesco pilot framework in 1984. The primary business-to-business (B2B) PC was made by Thomson Holidays in 1981.

In 1990, Tim Berners-Lee made the primary World Wide Web server and program. In 1992, Charles Stack made the main online book shop Book Stacks Unlimited,[xiv] two years before Jeff Bezos began Amazon.com. In 1994, different advances occurred, for example, web-based banking and the opening of an online pizza shop by Pizza Hut. During that year, Netscape presented SSL encryption (Secure Sockets Layer) of information moved on the web, which is basic for secure internet shopping. In 1995, Amazon extended its web-based shopping, and in 1996, eBay showed up.

Growth

Most of the earliest online customers were young, educated males who knew about PC innovation, yet by 2001, ladies made up 52.8 percent of the online population. Online shopping had grabbed the eye of the overall population by 1999, and both new companies and standard retailers had Web destinations offering their items. During the Christmas shopping period of 1999, so many buyers attempted to do their shopping on the web that retailers found themselves unprepared to process and ship their requests efficiently.

Online retailers improved their client care and transporting organizations; for example, FedEx and UPS extended their activities to oblige the expanding traffic. By December 2008, numerous online retailers had the option to support their deals by offering ensured medium-term conveyance to customers as late as on Christmas Eve.

Excitement over the capability of web-based retailing led ridiculous business desires during the dot.com bubble of 1999–2001. New companies attempted to sell items like staple goods and canine nourishment over the Internet without representing the restrictive expense of keeping up stockrooms and conveyance frameworks. Organizations with built-up retail locations, however, had the option to grow their client base utilizing the framework they previously had set up.

Clients

Online shopping requires access to a PC, and some form of payment, for example, a bank account, charge card, or PayPal account. As indicated by the *Journal of Electronic Commerce*, the higher the degree of training, pay, and control of the leader of the family unit, the more ideal the impression of non-store shopping. Expanded presentation to innovation builds the likelihood of creating positive dispositions towards new shopping channels. As the development of innovation has made PCs more affordable and accessible to more individuals and expanded the simplicity of interfacing with the Internet, the client base has extended.

The popularity of online shopping is a worldwide wonder. Reviews of Internet clients have uncovered that 99 percent of South Korean web clients have shopped on the web, followed by 97 percent of web clients in Germany, Japan, and the United Kingdom. Ninety-four percent of Internet clients in the United States revealed that they had bought something on the web. Utilizing a credit card to buy things on the Internet is particularly speaking to purchasers in developing markets who can work only with significant effort to find or purchase things they need in neighborhood retail locations.

Merchants

Numerous effective virtual retailers sell advanced items (counting data stockpiling, recovery, and change), music, motion pictures, instruction, correspondence, programming, photography, and monetary exchanges. Instances of this kind of organization include Google, eBay, and PayPal. Huge quantities of advertisers, remembering various venders for eBay, use drop delivery or offshoot showcasing methods to encourage exchanges of substantial products without keeping up genuine stock. Little things, for example, books, CDs, and gems that have a high worth and can fit into a standard envelope are especially appropriate for virtual stores.

The initial success of Amazon, maybe the oldest website organization, depended on selling things that were easy to send.

High-volume sites, for example, Yahoo!, Amazon.com, and eBay, offer facilitating services for online stores to small retailers. These stores are exhibited inside an incorporated structure. Collections of online stores are sometimes known as virtual shopping centers or online commercial centers.

Logistics

Buyers discover items by utilizing an internet searcher, visiting the website of the retailer directly, or doing a hunt crosswise over a wide range of sellers utilizing a shopping web index that offers cost and quality examinations.

Most online retailers use shopping basket programming that enables the client to choose numerous things to add to a request and alter quantity.

When the request is finished, the client travels through a checkout process during which payment and delivery data are gathered. A few stores enable shoppers to pursue an online account that keeps installment data and transportation addresses on permanent account with the goal that the checkout procedure can be mechanized. The purchaser normally observes a confirmation page and is sent an email confirmation once the exchange is finished. Extra messages tell the client when the request has been sent and may give follow-up data on the shipment.

Less sophisticated stores may show an inventory on their webpage and depend on purchasers to arrange payment and shipment by phone or email.

Payment

Online customers ordinarily use a charge card to make payments using:

- Debit card
- Various kinds of electronic cash
- Cash on delivery (COD, not offered by many online stores)
- Electronic bank check
- Wire delivery
- Postal cash request
- PayPal
- Google Checkout
- Amazon Payments
- Bill Me Later
- Money bookers
- Reverse SMS charging to cell phones

Understanding Digitalization

- Gift cards
- Direct charge in certain nations

A few dealers are not set up to ship abroad and won't permit global credit cards. The money-related piece of an exchange might be prepared continuously (for instance, telling the customer immediately that a Mastercard has been declined), or maybe done later as a component of the satisfaction procedure.

Item Delivery

When a payment has been acknowledged, the products or services can be delivered in various ways.

- Download: This is the technique regularly utilized for advanced media items, for example, programming, music, motion pictures, or images.
- Shipping: The item is delivered to the client's location.
- Postal administration: The dealer utilizes normal mail to send the item.
- Drop shipping: The request is passed to the maker or outsider merchant, who sends the thing directly to the shopper, bypassing the retailer's physical area to spare time, cash, and space.
- In-store pickup: The client requests and pays on the web, finds a nearby store utilizing locator programming, and goes to the nearest store. This is the technique regularly utilized in the bricks-and-clicks business model.
- If the purchase is a gift card, the client may get a numerical code or a ticket that can be printed out and displayed. To prevent duplication, a similar right of confirmation can't be utilized twice.

- Electronic registration: A client obtaining an airline ticket gets a confirmation email, and checks in at the air terminal by swiping a similar charge card or an identification at a stand.

Shopping Cart Frameworks

- Simple shopping cart frameworks don't utilize an online database. The shipper makes a disconnected database of items, classes, illustrations, and costs, and afterward transfers it to an internet shopping cart.

- Sophisticated shopping cart software can be purchased or leased as an independent program or as an expansion to a venture asset program. It is generally introduced without anyone else's Web server and might be coordinated into the organization's current inventory network framework, so requesting, installment, conveyance, bookkeeping, and satisfaction can be mechanized to a huge degree.

- A shipper can enroll and make an online shop on a gateway that has different shops and offers extra services, for example, credit card handling.

- Open-source shopping cart bundles incorporate propelled stages, for example, Interchange, and off-the-rack arrangements as osCommerce,[xv] Magento,[xvi] Zen Cart,[xvii] VirtueMart,[xviii] and PrestaShop.[xix] These can be custom-fitted to suit the dealer's needs.

Web Site Design

Clients pick web-based shopping due to its elevated level of comfort. For a retailer, a shopping website expands deals, builds client access to its items, and reinforces brand awareness and client loyalty. Great webpage configuration is significant to the achievement of a web-based shopping website.

Numerous retailers confront difficulties in making an engaging web-based shopping experience for their clients.

Online shopping sites give definite item data that isn't normally accessible in a retail location, alongside methods for effectively looking at the properties of a few comparable items. The measure of data and the manner by which it is introduced directly influences the client's tendency to purchase items and services on the web.

Two significant elements that have been found to impact purchasing conduct are complexity and curiosity. "Complexity" refers to the number of various components or highlights of a site; a site that shows similar data in a few distinct ways can drive purchases. "Curiosity" includes surprising, new, or new angles to a site, for example, week after week offers, occasional items, news stories, and pop-up windows. Oddity keeps clients investigating the shopping sites.

The client-focused plan is significant. The reason for a web-based shopping webpage is to form associations with clients and profit. The essential focal point of the website ought to be fulfilling the purchasers' desires, not supporting the association's way of life and brand name. Purchasers look for productivity, great client support, a feeling that the organization thinks about them, and a steady encounter each time they come back to the site. An association must contribute generous assets to characterize, plan, create, test, execute, and keep up a shopping webpage. Errors should be corrected when they are found. To keep clients, client support must return messages in a timely manner, tell clients of issues, be simple, and be a good steward of the clients' data. Internet deals can't be completely mechanized; an enormous number of online customers contact the organization by phone or email to pose questions before making a buy, and to determine issues subsequently.

The website design must take into consideration the social quirks and tastes of expected clients. Plan components that appeal to a Japanese or Chinese client may have the contrary impact on a German client. It is essential to make the data on a webpage accessible in the language of the clients to avoid false impressions and increase their trust in the product. A client's commonality with the web additionally influences behavior on a shopping website. Experienced clients center more around the factors that impact the job needing to be done, while learner clients focus on finding and understanding the data on a shopping site.

Online Shopping And Retail Shopping

Online shopping offers certain advantages and favorable circumstances, yet it will never supplant the experience of shopping in a retail location. A client who knows precisely what the person needs can find it on the web, read and think about the data, and buy from the webpage that offers the best cost or service. A customer who is questionable on what to search for, or who appreciates browsing through things in plain view, will lean toward a retail location where the product can be seen, dealt with, and inspected. The stylistic theme, music, and game plan of products in a retail location make a multi-dimensional shopping experience that can't be copied on the web. For some individuals, going out on the town to shop at a shopping center, retail establishment, or market is a type of excitement and social experience.

Numerous individuals who are new to PCs and don't feel good utilizing the Internet to shop are not liable to change their habits.

Online stores must portray items available to be purchased with content, photographs, and interactive media documents, while in a retail location, the genuine item and the producer's packaging are accessible for direct assessment, which may include a test drive, fitting, or other experimentation. In a regular retail location, agents are ordinarily accessible to respond to questions. A few things, such as apparel and shoes, have to be tried on before the client can be sure they are the correct size. Internet shopping destinations offer size graphs, charts, and multi-sided perspectives to enable the client to make a determination. Most offer liberal merchandise exchanges to entice clients to buy.

Online stores are available 24 hours per day, and numerous customers have Internet at both work and home. A visit to a traditional retail location requires travel and should occur during business hours. During the Christmas season and on weekends, customers in retail locations may have to fight with crowds and long lines.

Searching or browsing an online list can be quicker than perusing the passageways of a physical store. One favorable position of shopping on the web has the option to rapidly search out and think about costs for things or services from a wide range of merchants utilizing web indexes and online value correlation services. In certain markets, for example, books and music, PCs, and buyer hardware, customers can locate a more noteworthy determination online and might have the option to find restored or recycled things at much lower costs.

Collectors and hobbyists can find supplies and uncommon things online that are infrequently accessible in retail locations and can utilize closeout destinations to sell, exchange, and research collectibles, antiques, and stand-out pieces. Forte items, for example, ethnic nourishments and wines, outside gear, and outdoor supplies, are also sold at focused costs on the web. Web-based shopping is also an effective method to purchase car parts and new parts for machines, since it is hard for a retail outlet to keep them in stock.

Some online stores give supplemental item data, for example, directions, wellbeing methods, exhibits, maker determinations, counsel, or how-to guides. Many shopping locales enable clients to rate their things. There are also committed survey locales that host client audits for various items.

Shipping

Much of the time, stock obtained online must be transported to the client. This introduces a significant delay and potential vulnerability about whether the thing was in stock at the hour of procurement. Regardless of whether a purchase can be made 24 hours a day, the client should frequently be at home during ordinary business hours to accept the delivery.

In case of an issue with the item, the client may need to contact the retailer, visit the mail station, and pay return transportation, and then wait for a substitution or discount.

Delivery costs (if relevant) diminish the favorable value position of an online product. Online retailers sometimes make a profit by charging a standard transportation expense that surpasses the real cost of delivery the thing.

Brick-and-click stores offer the capacity to purchase a thing on the web and get it in a nearby store. Requests are filled promptly with the goal that they are prepared before the client has the opportunity to land at the store. This element gives retail locations a focused edge over other online retailers who may offer lower costs but must send out product, and fulfills clients who need their merchandise right away. It also brings online clients onto the store premises where they may purchase extra products or look for help with an item.

Trends

A huge number of individuals that shop online utilize an internet searcher to discover what they are searching for while others discover sites by listening in on others' conversations. Numerous customers react to uncommon ideas in messages and publicizing, or discover a dealer through a value correlation website.

Trust is a significant factor in choosing an online shopper. Sixty percent of online customers who have a decent first involvement with a specific webpage come back to that site to purchase more. A setup retailer with a notable brand is bound to be trusted more than an unknown merchant.

Books and music are the most well-known online purchases, trailed by garments and frill, shoes, recordings and DVDs, games, aircraft tickets, and electronic hardware. Beautifying agents, nourishment items, and food supplies are progressively being bought on the web. Around one-fourth of travelers purchase their plane tickets online because it is a brisk and simple approach to analyze carrier travel and make a buy.

Numerous effective virtual organizations manage computerized items (counting data stockpiling, recovery, and alteration), music, motion pictures, office supplies, instruction, correspondence, programming, photography, and money related exchanges. Instances of this kind of organization include Google, eBay, and PayPal. Other effective advertisers use drop delivering or associate showcasing methods to encourage exchanges of merchandise without keeping up genuine stock. Models remember various merchants for eBay.

Brick-and-mortar retailers regularly utilize their internet shopping locales to drive deals both on the web and at their retail locations by posting data about in-store specials on the web and by offering free additional items, for example, batteries or assistance to clients who investigate items on their Web destinations.

Concerns

Fraud and Security Concerns

Online customers have a greater danger of being swindled by a shipper since they can't physically look at the stock before obtaining it. Dishonest dealers, at times, accept payment for a request and never send the product. Most charge card administrations offer assurance against this kind of fraud. Traders additionally chance losses from purchases made utilizing stolen charge cards or fraudulent repudiation of online purchases.

Secure Sockets Layer (SSL) encryption prevents charge card numbers from being caught in travel between the purchaser and the dealer. Fraud is a worry for customers if programmers break into a dealer's site and take names, locations, and charge card numbers. PC security is a significant worry for vendors and internet business specialist organizations who deploy countermeasures, for example, firewalls and anti-virus software, to ensure their systems.

Phishing, in which shoppers are tricked into thinking they are dealing with a respectable retailer, are fooled into giving private data to a noxious gathering, which is another peril. Denial of service attacks is a minor hazard for vendors, as are server and system blackouts.

Customers can secure themselves when utilizing web retailer services by:

- using known stores, guaranteeing that there are far-reaching contact data on the site before utilizing the service, and taking note of whether the retailer has joined up with industry oversight projects, for example, trust mark or a trust seal.

- ensuring that the retailer has posted a protection strategy expressing that it won't impart private data to others without consent.

- ensuring that the seller address is ensured with SSL (see above) when entering financial data; the URL of the charge card data passage screen should begin with "HTTPS."

- using solid passwords that exclude individual data, for example, names or birthdates.

- reading autonomous buyer surveys of individual encounters with an organization or item, which can frequently be found by typing the organization name into a web search tool.

- confirming that extraordinary ideas in messages or web-based publicizing are real by going directly to the trader's webpage.

Most organizations offer transportation protection if an item is lost or harmed; if a thing is especially significant, the client ought to confirm that it is guaranteed.

Privacy

The security of individual data is important to certain buyers. Lawful purviews have various laws concerning purchaser protection and various degrees of authorization. Numerous buyers wish to avoid spam and telemarketing, which could come about from providing contact data to an online merchant. Most traders vow not to utilize buyer data for these reasons. Retail locations also gather buyer data. Some request locations and telephone numbers at the sales register, though shoppers may decline to give it. Bigger organizations, some of the time, utilize the location data encoded on buyers' credit cards to add them to an index mailing list.

The Dos And Don'ts In Online Shopping

If individuals need to be shrewd online customers and avoid turning into a victim of cybercrime, clients need to pursue a couple of essential do's and don'ts when purchasing from sites.

DOs:

- Before giving the charge card data, enough time must be taken to investigate the site. Contact the merchant if this is the client's first buy. Most trustworthy sellers will have a cost-free client assistance telephone number. If the site has just an email address and no telephone number, start an email or text exchange with the individuals running the site before purchasing anything from them.

- Pay with a credit card or online payment service. Online payment service offers some security too. For an additional level of security, a credit card is the best.

- Buy from a site that has encryption. "Encryption is key to verify Internet buys. It is a component that consequently codes the client's close to home information when it is entered".

- Check the site strategies before submitting the request. Peruse the site's arrival arrangement and different terms and conditions, just as the site's security strategy, before requesting anything.

- Use complete PC security software. Ensure the clients have up-to-date, comprehensive security software, for example, MCA expense Internet security or MCA charge Total assurance before doing anything with web-based shopping. This will lessen the danger of contracting an infection and will reduce the chance of robbery on risky sites.

Check the financial records to ensure that the client was charged the correct sum and that no additional items were put on their tab.

DON'TS:

- Do not purchase from spammers. If the client gets an email welcoming them to purchase something like "Limited Rolex Watches," two things must be considered.

Benefits of Shopping Online

1. Convenience. Convenience is the greatest advantage. What other place can you serenely shop at noon while in your pajamas? There are no lines to hold up in or clerks to find to assist you with your purchases, and you can do your shopping in minutes. Online shops offer us the chance to shop every minute of every day and reward us with a "no contamination" shopping experience. There is no better spot to purchase educational items like digital books, which are accessible to you in a flash. Downloadable things acquired online remove the requirement for any sort of physical material whatsoever, which helps the earth!

2. Better costs. Better costs are accessible on the web, since items come to you direct from the maker or dealer without including go-betweens. Also, it's simpler to think about costs and locate a superior arrangement. Numerous online destinations offer markdown coupons and discounts, too. In addition to the fact that prices are better, you can save money on a sales tax also, since online shops are possibly required to gather a business tax if they have a physical area

in your state. Factor in the spared cost of gas, and you have saved yourself a great deal of cash!

3. More variety. The decisions online are astonishing. You can discover practically any brand or thing you're searching for. You can get in on the most recent global patterns without burning through cash on airfare. You can shop from retailers in different areas of the state, nation, or even world, as opposed to being constrained by your topography. A far more noteworthy choice of hues and sizes than you will discover locally are available to you. Besides, the stock is substantially more plentiful, so you'll generally have the option to locate your size and color. Some online shops even acknowledge orders for out-of-stock things and ship when they come in.

4. You can send gifts all the more effectively. Sending gifts to family members and companions is simple, regardless of where they are. All the packaging and sending is achieved for you. Periodically, they'll even gift wrap it for you! Presently, there is no compelling reason to come up with a rationalization for not sending a present on events like birthday events, weddings, anniversaries, Valentine's Day, Mother's Day, Father's Day, etc.

5. More control. Commonly, when we choose regular shopping, we will, in general, spend significantly more than arranged and wind up purchasing things that aren't actually what we needed. On the web, you don't need to let the store's stock direct what you purchase, and you can get precisely what you need.

6. Easy value examinations. Contrasting and exploring items and their costs are a lot simpler on the web. If you're looking for tools, for instance, you can discover purchaser surveys and item examinations for every one of the choices available, with connections to the best costs. We can inquire

Understanding Digitalization

about the firsthand experience, appraisals, and surveys for most items and retailers.

7. No crowds. Particularly during holidays or weekends, crowds can be a pain. Additionally, being squashed in the hordes of customers once in a while makes us feel rushed. You don't need to fight for a parking place.

8. No outside influence. Sometimes when we're out shopping, we wind up purchasing things we don't generally require, all because retailers pressure us or utilize their offering abilities to urge us to make these purchases.

9. You can purchase used or damaged things at lower costs. The commercial center on the Internet gives us access to postings of old or damaged things at absolute bottom costs. Also, if we want to buy antiques, there's no better place to find great ones.

10. Discreet purchases are simpler. A few things are better done in the protection of your home. Online shops are best for prudent purchases for things like grown-up toys, attractive unmentionables, etc. This empowers us to buy underpants and undergarments without shame or any neurosis that there are people watching or passing judgment on us.

Disadvantages of Online Shopping

1. The negative effect of packaging. Having your purchase stuffed in a few layers of plastic and cardboard and conveyed right to your front entryway is beneficial for you, however, not all that good for nature. Regardless of whether you attempt to reuse the cardboard, you're making pointless waste by shopping on the web.

2. Shipping issues and delays. Indeed, even the greatest and best-transporting organizations and online retailers have their awful days, so there's no real way to guarantee that

you'll get your hands on your purchase in time unless you get it from a store. Things get lost, bypassed, harmed, or conveyed to an inappropriate location more regularly than you can imagine.

3. Risk of fraud. If you're shopping on the web, there's a bigger risk of fraud: charge card tricks, phishing, hacking, data fraud, fake items, bogus sites, and different tricks are normal.

4. Spending a lot of time on the web. Particularly if your activity necessitates that you take a gander at a PC throughout the day, you may get worn out on all that screen time. Shopping on the web can transform into a long-distance race of looking over and clicking down rabbit holes, and before you know it, you've been online for the greater part of the day. The web is a decent spot to visit. However, you most likely would prefer not to live there.

5. Less contact with the network. If you do all your business on the web, you'll never need to leave your home. This may be incredible for a spell; however, in some cases, you should head outside, inhale some natural air, get a difference in view, converse with genuine individuals, take an interest in your locale, and be a piece of the group. At times, a PC screen can't contend with a genuine human association.

6. You don't know precisely what you're getting. Unless you are personally familiar with a brand or item, purchasing on the web requires an act of pure trust, one that doesn't generally end in support of you. Sizes are frequently uncertain. You can't decide surface, texture, fit, cut, quality, heft, or durability just by taking a gander at a photograph. Items that looked extraordinary may feel shoddy, unbalanced, or modest when you grasp them.

7. Returns can be confusing. A few dealers make the procedure easy; however, many make it extra difficult for you to return their product or get a discount. Commonly, you can't get repaid for any transportation costs. Labeling, packaging, transporting, following, and rounding out all the best possible structures is an issue you can stay away from if you purchase face-to-face (and if you hand-select your product, you won't have to return things so regularly).

8. Unfriendly, shifty, or confusing sites. A few destinations necessitate that you join their mailing list and make it difficult to withdraw. Some sell your email address to other people, so your email is loaded with promotions. Here and there, destinations don't offer great or precise portrayals of the products, or you can't make sense of how to buy or restore a thing or address client care.

9. No deals help. In a store, there's normally somebody to help you; however, on the web, you're alone. If you're befuddled or have questions, it's simply not good enough for you. You may need to make blind purchases and errors you'll lament later in light of the fact that there was nobody to converse with.

10. No help for nearby retailers. If everybody began doing all their shopping on the web, all the neighborhood stores would go out of business. At the point when every one of the stores around is gone, we'll need to drive further and find away to shop at a genuine store. Numerous individuals and businesses have just encountered the negative, and now and again crushing, effects of internet business, which removes occupations and devastates local economies.

Chapter 7

Digital Economy

The digital economy is the overall system of monetary exercises, business exchanges, and expert cooperation that are empowered by information and communications technologies (ICT).

It tends to be compactly summarized as the economy dependent on digital technologies.

Wear Tapscott first authored the term *digital economy* in a 1995 top-rated book *The Digital Economy: Promise and Peril in the Age of Networked Intelligence.*

Nicholas Negroponte, the organizer of the Massachusetts Institute of Technology's Media Lab and writer of the 1995 book *Being Digital*, has depicted the digital economy as utilizing "bits rather than atoms."

Digital Economy vs. Internet Economy

In its early days, the digital economy was called the new economy, or the web economy, because of its dependence on web availability. However, economists and business leaders assert that the digital economy is further developed and complex than the web economy, which, under one definition, basically implies financial worth gotten from the web.

The digital economy mirrors the move from the third mechanical transformation to the fourth industrial revolution. The third industrial revolution, in some cases called the digital revolution, refers to the progressions that occurred in the late twentieth century with the change from simple electronic and mechanical gadgets to digital technologies.

The fourth mechanical upheaval expands on the digital revolution as technologies today keep on connecting the physical and cyber worlds.

Significance of the Digital Economy

Although a few associations and people use innovations to execute existing errands on the PC, the digital economy is further developed than that. It isn't just utilizing a PC to perform tasks customarily done physically or on simple gadgets. Rather, the digital economy features the chance for associations and people to utilize innovations to execute those undertakings better, quicker, and frequently uniquely in contrast to previously. Also, the term mirrors the capacity to use innovations to execute tasks and take part in exercises that weren't conceivable previously. Such open doors for existing substances to improve, to achieve more, to do things any other way, and to do new things, are enveloped in the related idea of digital change.

Digital Technologies

The digital economy broadens well past digitization and robotization. Rather, this new worldview tackles numerous trend-setting innovations and innovation stages. Those advances and stages incorporate, yet aren't restricted to, hyperconnectivity, the internet of things (IoT), huge amounts of information, progressed investigation, remote systems, cell phones, and online life.

The digital economy utilizes these innovations, both independently and in the show, to adjust customary trades and empower new ones.

Entrepreneurs in the Digital Economy

Various business visionaries seized on the technologies that fuel the digital economy to make new organizations and new plans of action that couldn't have existed, or existed at the size and scale they do today, in past ages. These new organizations incorporate the ride-sharing companies Uber and Lyft, the home rental business Airbnb, and substance-on-request benefits, for example, Netflix and Spotify.

Digital Transformation Examples

There are various instances of traditional organizations changing to prevail in the digital economy. Take retailers, for instance. Most retailers at first created sites to empower online deals. As the world moves all the more completely into the digital economy, groundbreaking retailers presently influence technologies to reach and serve clients through a variety of channels. These retailers utilize online deals and portable applications to distinguish purchasers, regardless of whether they're shopping through the web or face-to-face. They can gather and examine every client's perusing and deals information to all the more likely understand their inclinations. Furthermore, they can utilize that information to connect with clients through web-based life, taking into consideration better help and, ultimately, higher sales and increased brand loyalty.

Utilizing innovation to bind together the client experience crosswise over various genuine world and cyberspaces is frequently called an omni-channel or multichannel approach.

Another case of advanced change is John Deere, the 179-year-old organization based on making ranch gear that presently additionally incorporates information-driven stages to assist farmers in optimizing production.

Vehicle producers that offer telematics answers to pinpoint and convey upkeep prerequisites, for example, Daimler Trucks North America and its Detroit Connect Virtual Technician, which gives remote analytic support of select tracks, additionally outline the digital change expected to contend in the digital economy.

Rushes of Interruption

The digital economy has made rushes of disturbance. New organizations and better approaches for associating have developed. Notwithstanding, numerous organizations and projects that didn't or couldn't profit by the innovations to change their activities have confronted declining deals, falling shares of the overall industry, and even total breakdown.

The taxi business is presently attempting to go after clients who discover Uber and Lyft simpler to utilize. Kodak and other camera hardware organizations that didn't move to digital formats and internet sharing stages shrank their item contributions as cell phones and online life stages supplanted film and photograph collections.

The Future of the Digital Economy

Business specialists concur that the digital economy is at its beginning.

To contend in the years ahead, associations, regardless of whether they are revenue-driven organizations, service-situated—for example, medicinal services frameworks—or charitable and government establishments, will require the two heads and workers who can enhance.

How Should We Measure the Digital Economy?

In 2018, Americans spent 6.3 hours daily on digital media, Google, and Wikipedia, as well as interpersonal organizations, online courses, maps, informing, videoconferencing, music, and cell phone applications. Digital media expends an enormous and developing portion of our cognizant existence, yet the merchandise and products go uncounted in legitimate measures of economic activity, for example, GDP and efficiency (which is essentially GDP every hour worked). We tune in to more and better music, explore easily, speak with collaborators and companions in a rich assortment of ways, and appreciate hordes of different advantages we couldn't have imagined 40 years ago. Yet, if you somehow happened to take a gander at GDP numbers, you'd imagine that the computerized transformation never occurred. The contribution of the data part as a portion of absolute GDP has scarcely moved since the 1980s, floating somewhere in the range of 4% and 5% every year and arriving at a high of just 5.5% in 2018.

The estimation of advanced contributions is underrepresented in that GDP depends on what individuals pay for merchandise and projects. With barely any exceptions, if something has a cost of zero, at that point, it contributes zero to GDP. The majority of us get more of an incentive from free advanced merchandise, for example, Wikipedia and online maps, than we did from their progressively costly paper predecessors.

Strategy producers use GDP information to settle on choices about how to put resources into everything from foundation and R & D to instruction and cyberdefense. Controllers use it to set an approach that influences innovation firms and different associations. Since the advantages of digitization are significantly underestimated, those choices and strategies are being made with a poor understanding of reality.

Effective management of the digital economy relies upon our capacity to precisely survey the estimation of free digital merchandise and projects. That is the reason we built up another procedure to quantify not just how much purchasers pay for digital items, but the amount they profit by them. Also, that uncounted advantage is generous. For instance, our examination with Felix Eggers, of the University of Groningen, found that Facebook alone has made more than $225 billion worth of uncounted value for shoppers since 2004.

Catching the unmeasured advantage of free products is certainly another issue: Think of prior floods of development that created free and almost free contributions, like anti-infection agents, radio, and TV, which delivered significant value to the shopper. Given the uncommonly fast development of digital goods and services in our economy, it's past time to take care of this issue.

What GDP Doesn't Measure

Gross domestic product is regularly utilized as an intermediary for how the economy is getting along. It's a generally exact number that flags each quarter as to whether the economy is developing or contracting.

Since it quantifies just the amount we pay for things, not the amount we advantage, customer's financial prosperity may not be connected with GDP. It sometimes falls when GDP goes up, and the other way around. The gross domestic product can be a deceptive intermediary for financial well-being.

Fortunately, financial matters provide a way, from a certain perspective, to measure consumer well-being. That measure is called *purchaser excess*, which is the contrast between the most extreme a buyer would pay for a product or service and its cost. If you would have spent as much as $100 for a shirt yet paid just $40, at that point, you have a $60 purchaser excess.

To comprehend why GDP can be a deceptive intermediary for economic well-being, consider Encyclopedia Britannica and Wikipedia. Britannica used to cost a few thousand dollars, which means its clients believed it to be worth that sum. Wikipedia, free assistance, has undeniably more articles than Britannica ever did.

Estimated by customer spending, the industry is contracting (the print reference book left the business in 2012 as shoppers abandoned it). Our exploration found that the middle value that US shoppers place on Wikipedia is about $150 per year, yet the expense is $0. That converts into generally $42 billion in buyer surplus that isn't reflected in the US gross domestic product. Purchaser spending, the reason for GDP, can be tallied at the sales register and appears on organizations' income proclamations.

Interestingly, customer surplus can't be straightforwardly watched, which is one reason it hasn't been utilized much for estimating the economy. Luckily, digital transformation has made incredible new estimation tools. In our exploration, we utilize digital overview methods to run gigantic online decision tests looking at the inclinations of countless shoppers. The outcomes enable us to evaluate the purchaser surplus for an incredible assortment of merchandise, including free ones that are absent from GDP measurements.

We start by requesting that members settle on decisions. Now and again, we request that they pick between different merchandise (for instance, "Would you rather lose access to Wikipedia or Facebook for one month?"). In others, they pick between holding access to a digital great or surrendering it in return for money-related remuneration ("Would you surrender Wikipedia for a month for $10?"). To ensure that individuals have uncovered their actual inclinations, we catch up with tests in which members really should surrender something before they can get paid.

(1) Taxation

Information-related organizations are new, dynamic, and universal. Step-by-step instructions to consolidate them in the current residential approach system is a major test. One of the questionable issues is tax assessment.

One issue is on value-added taxes (VAT). Numerous nations apply VAT that is gathered from venders. There is a contention that local specialist co-ops may become disadvantaged contrasted with remote specialist organizations through the web that are not dependent upon such assessments. On this issue, numerous nations have pursued the proposals gave by BEPS Action 1 on Digital Economy22 and have implemented an instrument for gathering VAT on services obtained by private purchasers from non-occupant providers/merchants (if conceivable) or the shoppers on payment.

Another increasingly controversial issue is corporate, and personal assessments. The customary standard is that mode 1 (cross-fringe) specialist co-ops are dealt with like product exporters and accordingly pay corporate income taxes in the home country, not in export-destination countries where giant international platforms procure benefits that aren't extremely clear. How they structure and work isn't regularly broadcast in detail. There is a concern concerning their expense exchange rehearses that exploit charge rate contrasts crosswise over nations to keep away from charge payments.

Individuals additionally stress over a potential disadvantageous situation of residential platforms that cover annual corporate assessments versus monster platforms who may not pay a lot. To address such concerns, discourses were held under the Inclusive Framework on BEPS to locate a planned answer for this issue.

At the same time, various nations have begun presenting or considering supposed break measures to impose digital benefits on remote platforms regularly as tax collection on the measure of offers, under the conviction that it is basic to act rapidly.

The logic of interim measures is somewhat reasonable, however dubious. Monetarily, such duties have an impact, like the instance of exchange merchandise where a duty is forced prejudicially on explicit exporters. By what means can a province distinguish the duty-owing gatherings and their suitable degree of tax collection? The discussion encompassing these issues is critical.

There should be no particular tax assessment on the advanced economy. It ought to be exhausted as some other action altogether not to decrease the free streams in trade. As prescribed previously, orchestrated nexus and benefit allotment ideas ought to be applied by the exigencies of digitalization. At last, as increasingly more monetary action shifts on the web, the basics of technological neutrality in applying assessments will turn out to be progressively critical.

(2) E-payments, Fin-tech, and Other Mechanical Guidelines

E-payments are thriving in numerous recently created and developing nations and are diminishing transaction costs as a strong substitute to conventional installment frameworks. The basic mechanical advancement in biometric confirmation, AI, blockchain, online credit scoring, and peer-to-peer (P2P) financing is among the worldwide patterns of fin-tech improvement. Step-by-step instructions to join these new digital services into the arrangement of fiscal and money-related guidelines is an earnest point.

The authorizing framework or wellbeing models for transportation services, lodging services, and others is another issue for how to fuse new digital services into the conventional services structure.

(3) AI

Consolidating new advances into our economy and society is constantly a major test. One significant theme is AI.

The OECD Committee on Digital Economy Policy set up an Expert Group on Artificial Intelligence in Society (AIGO) in May 2018, to scope standards for open arrangement and universal participation. The as of now proposed Guidelines for AI incorporate five standards: comprehensive and practical development and prosperity, human-focused qualities and reasonableness, straightforwardness and logic, strength and security, and accountability.

(4) Information Disclosure of Firms and Measurements

A key issue is that the data on the giant universal platforms isn't all revealed. Outcasts have little ability to see how they sort out and work their exercises locally and globally, where they have servers to store the information, and how they benefit. These issues have made a progression of worries on universal digital organizations, especially with regards to rivalry arrangement, tax assessment, and insights. A potential cure is to present an arrangement of data exposure for their exercises.

(5) Due Procedure in Government Access to Security/Industry Information

Another worry in the advanced economy is how and to what degree the service can access private or industry information. In numerous nations, the police can enter a privately owned business or living arrangement to examine through appropriate legitimate fair treatment accommodate in their legal framework. On the internet, such rules appear to be obscured. Sooner or later, we may need to present an appropriate fair treatment for government intercession.

6. Mechanical Policy and Strategic Trade and Investment Policies

Against the foundation of the above contemplations concerning the governance of information, maybe the most troublesome issue confronting the G20 is that of key exchange and venture strategy boosted by the rents accessible in the worldwide area in the information-driven economy. Newborn child enterprises, or, better, new problematic plans of action are developing in the IoT space. All the significant wards are contributing heavily to verify their solid footing and addition upper hand. This isn't an awful thing: the reason for open interest in this area is strong given the high risks included, the quickness of innovative change, which alters the skyline for the recuperation of ventures, and the potential social advantages of new advancements, which may far surpass private returns.

Anyway, as in earlier occasions when new advances made such chances, the key exchange and speculation strategy are prompting an exchange war. While the primary activity has been between the major innovative forces, and specifically between the United States and China, it is normal for recently created and developing economies to also think about supporting their very own businesses behind digital firewalls, with national online business methodologies. Is it financially legitimate?

We can apply standard contention on newborn child industry insurance, even on account of information-related organizations. To begin with, check whether the business will be universally focused toward the end (Mill's standard). Second, check whether the time-limited future advantages would be bigger than the time-limited costs (Bastable's basis). At that point, confirm whether government intervention is fundamental, the trial of the presence of externalities.

7. The Way Ahead

The foundation of an effective supporting strategy system for the digital economy is critical, especially for recently developed and developing countries. To set a "free progression of information" as a default is a helpful way to deal with looking at supporting arrangements in an efficient way. The arrangement of strategies for the progression of information and information-related organizations must be neither too powerless nor too strong. G20 might need to attempt a thorough stocktaking of approaches identified with information streams and information-related organizations.

The launch of new chats on new internet business leads in the WTO is uplifting news, which G20 might need to help. Thinking about the degree of preparedness in supporting approaches in different nations, a nation might need to be particular in picking its remote partners. In a perfect world, we might want to set up an all-encompassing multilateral system. However, this will require significant investment. Recently created and developing nations may need to figure out how to experience progression rapidly to appreciate the advantages of the digital economy and improve global intensity.

The web has energetically become a private, decentralized activity, as opposed to following a top-down approach by governments. Cell phones and CT additionally have strong qualities of inclusiveness and have far-reaching impacts for different partners. Along these lines, in the coming residential and worldwide standard making for the progression of information and information-related organizations, we have to apply a multi-partner approach, including privately owned businesses, academics, and common society.

The new digital economy has become a key driver of United States monetary development and profitability. For example, the genuine worth included has developed at a normal yearly pace of 7.2% in recent years, multiple times quicker than GDP. The recent raft of innovative advances has also prompted the rise of deflationary value elements among digital goods and services. This has enabled an ever-increasing number of organizations to grasp new digital that improves corporate effectiveness, for example, the Internet of Things or distributed computing. Organizations in the digital period can work quicker and at a lower cost.

In spite of the undeniable boost from digital developments, US profitability development has eased back pointedly since the mid-2000s, which is a Catch-22. From 2014 to 2018, the government's legitimate work profitability measure has increased 1% every year, a rate normally connected with financial downturns as opposed to extensions.

Could improvements in measurable techniques uncover exactly how significant the digital economy is to financial success?

The Underrated Boost from the Digital Economy

New information from the Department of Commerce offers some significant bits of knowledge into the financial advantages of the digital economy. In 2017, the digital part represented 7% of ostensible GDP, a bigger offer than numerous customary areas, for example, retail exchange (5.6%) or development (4.0%). Since it is developing a lot quicker than the general economy, its commitment to GDP development has been outsized: The genuine digital economy represented nearly 30% of general US development in 2017 (Chart 1).

The lift from the digital divide has not exclusively been constrained to yield, yet has additionally separated into profitability. Over the previous decade, profitability in the digital economy has, by and large, developed twice as quickly as total efficiency (1.1% versus 0.5%, separately). In 2016, the digital economy's certain commitment to efficiency development relieved the total profitability decrease.

Digital price deflation is another appearance of how the advanced economy is giving a lift to profitability and financial development. Though costs in customary divisions of the economy would in general increase in ongoing decades, costs in the digital area have unwaveringly declined. In 2017, the cost deflator for the general economy expanded by 1.9% year over year, while that of the digital economy declined by 2.2%.

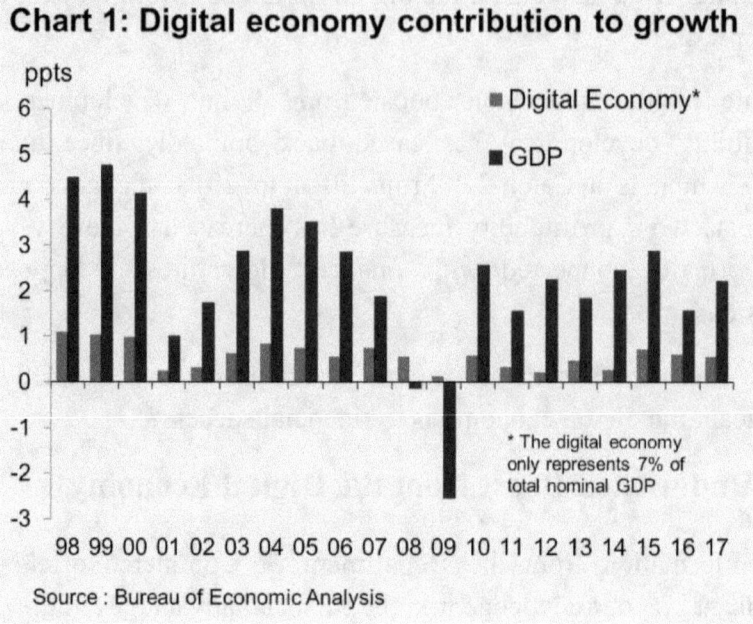

Source: Bureau of Economic Analysis

Measure correctly

One clarification that financial experts use to clarify languid total profitability development in the post-downturn period is mismeasurement: the possibility that official insights are unequipped for catching efficiency gains in IT-related products and projects. In such a manner, the most basic issues identify with the estimation of cost and quality change. If official value measures don't precisely catch quality improvements, value deflators are likely overestimated, and hence, genuine monetary yield is also likely underestimated.

Encouragingly, statistical agencies are progressively embracing hedonic measures to catch the utility of items and administrations, and the utilization of coordinating items strategies to guarantee comparative items with comparable quality are utilized crosswise over time.

Another estimation issue identifies with the changing organization of a quickly evolving economy. Regardless of whether it is organizations presenting new items and services, utilization substitution, or quality improvements, these advancements can make inclination evaluations of GDP and work profitability development descending. Anecdotal evidence outlines how an ever-increasing number of services, for example, Airbnb and Uber, are changing the economy in a way that might be progressively difficult to catch through legitimate insights. While it is incredibly hard to assess the efficiency development predisposition from these financial changes, it is very certain that these advancements have both supported profitability development and picked up in significance over the previous decade.

As David Byrne, John G. Fernald, and Marshall Reinsdorf brought up in a 2017 report, the mismeasurement challenge was at that point present before the log jam, and there is no proof that it has exacerbated after some time. Or maybe, major auxiliary obstructions—advances, moderate appropriation and dispersion through the economy, specifically—are keeping the digital economy from contributing a lot of a lift to profitability.

The Missing Link

In 1987, Robert Solow, the Nobel Prize-winning business analyst, broadly kidded that "you can see the PC age all over, however in the profitability measurements." At the time, yearly work efficiency development had eased back pointedly to around 0.5% in spite of significant advances in IT. The answer for Solow's Catch-22 came in the next decade, when work efficiency flooded back above 2% as an ever-increasing number of firms utilized IT advances to change how they work. In that light, the efficiency droop in the course of the most recent decade isn't such a great amount because of an absence of transformative developments; not so much a lack of transformative innovations, but more about a lack of innovation diffusion between firms and industries.

Inspecting firm-level efficiency development all around the general stoppage in yearly profitability development has transcendently influenced profitability laggards, which are firms that have a slower pace of innovative reception. In the meantime, worldwide frontier firms (top 50 firms, in part) have kept encountering moderately strong development. For example, information from Dan Andrews, Chiara Criscuolo, and Peter N. Lady in a 2016 report show that profitability development in the services segment has been multiple times quicker in the worldwide efficiency outskirt firms than in loafer firms since 2000.

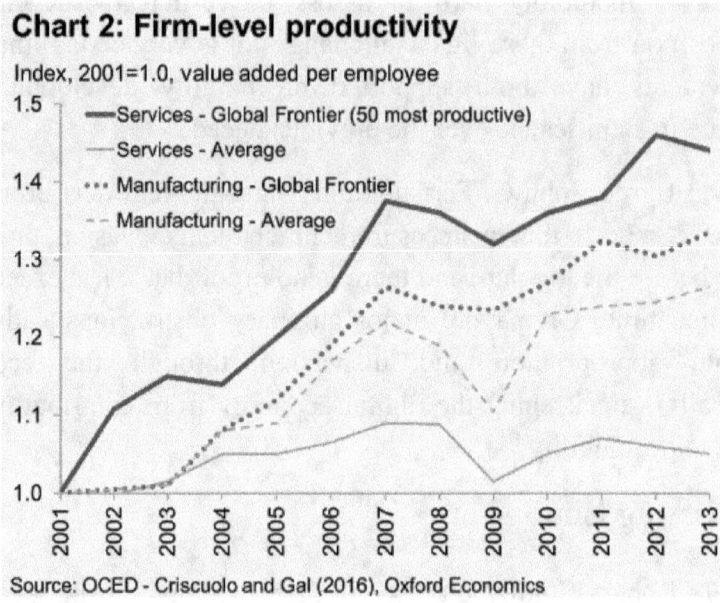

Source: OCED - Criscuolo and Gal (2016), Oxford Economics

The Next Productivity Boom

Undoubtedly, the lack of diffusion is not irreversible; there is space for idealism about the potential for the digital economy to help more grounded efficiency development. Approach changes could spike an increase in progressively far-reaching innovations: explicitly, arrangements that digital expanded challenge in item markets and lower hindrances to section, energize higher non-tangible investments, and support adequate training to enable new technologies. Also, a look back at past times of advancement uncovers that there has been a critical deferral between the commencement of innovations and their dispersion through the economy. That is particularly valid for sweeping mechanical developments, additionally called broadly useful innovations (GPTs, for example, the steam engine, power, and the PC).

It is hard to foresee when the next efficiency blast will happen, yet it could take some time—it took up to 30 years with past GPTs.

The Advantages and Difficulties of the Digital Economy for Developing Countries

First-order Benefits

The advantages of the digital economy for rising economies are conceivably enormous. That is because it can have huge intensity and profitability boosting identified with access to digital products and services that help enhance procedures and creation, lessen exchange costs, and change supply chains. Declining information and communication technology (ICT) costs energize venture and selection of digital advancements in developing economies, furnishing their organizations with frontline administrations at focused costs. The entirety of this empowers firms to take part in worldwide worth chains and legitimately get to clients in remote markets in manners already possible for huge and built-up organizations from cutting-edge economies.

For consumers, the advantages are related to access to a more extensive scope of products and enterprises at aggressive costs. It also offers new open doors for business enterprise and employment creation.

Governments also gain advantage from the digital economy to the degree that they approach advancements that assist them with conveying more and better open services, improve service, assess strategies, and convey better outcomes.

However, numerous digital economy benefits have not yet appeared at scale, which is because of adoption barriers, lag effects, transition costs, and digital commoditization. It is broadly concurred that governments of rising economies need to take a shot to empower the digital progress and receive the related rewards. These zones of mediation incorporate diminishing limitations and improving skills; interests in ICT biological systems, availability, and digital foundation;

understandings to advance ICT appropriation and dispersion; regulatory structures that encourage rivalry and economic situations; and arrangements to support investment and innovation.

These policy agendas are critical to quickening innovation appropriation and lessening advanced partitions in developing economies, which will have certain beneficial outcomes on firms, shoppers, and governments.

There is also advancement identified with the computerized economy that must be considered, of which the most significant is digital commoditization and the false notion of organization. It is sensible to assume, for instance, that the expanding cooperation of small- and medium-sized endeavors in internet business are probably going to decrease negligible advantages.

Digital commoditization could likewise check the overarching model of divided creation. As expressed, digital innovations are revising the conditions and geology of creation, and they empower the production on a focused premise of modern and straightforward merchandise, for instance, sports shoes and T-shirts. This is probably going to upset markets for an exceptionally subordinate articles of clothing providers, for example, El Salvador and Bangladesh, with these innovations behind the called "reshoring," that is, the arrival in cutting-edge nations of mechanical plants beforehand working in minimal effort economies.

Second-order benefits

In this new worldwide setting, it is essential to recognize "use" from "improvement, distribution, and management" of digital technologies. While most organizations are unimportant clients of digital commodities, a lot of littler offer falls into the class of engineers, merchants, and directors of those innovations. The on-screen characters in this last class are the ones characterizing the models and the stages on which advanced items and cross-fringe exchanges are worked and utilized.

Countries that have firms going about as designers of stages and managers of digital innovations are those well on the way to receiving the subsequent rewards that emerge from the digital economy, for example, better prospects as far as long-term development, employment and riches creation, and enduring beneficial outcomes on profitability and aggressiveness. Their populaces and firms are those that will, in general, benefit the most from the backhanded impacts of being in a more extravagant, open, and innovative environment.

Without a doubt, organizations such as Google, Amazon, Apple, Microsoft, Facebook, Baidu, Alibaba, SAP, PayPal, AT&T, Uber, Tencent, Cisco, Oracle, Huawei, Siemens, Bosch, and others, are creating advanced gadgets and stages in which third organizations work utilizing predefined models inside a given system. Shortening innovation lifecycles alongside system and stage impacts are setting up an exceptionally asymmetric winner-takes-all model in which the superstars have the upper hand, keeping them well in front of digital commodity clients.

In spite of the fact that support in e-commerce platforms enables firms from rising economies to hypothetically interact with a great many purchasers around the world, nearness in such stages isn't nonpartisan. A blockbuster factor joined with other unfair practices strengthen the calculation impact that drives buyers to the most researched about firms and things. Accordingly, worldwide e-commerce businesses give a long tail of sellers. However, just a chosen few are probably going to be successful.

The rivalry might be constrained by discriminatory arrangements, including non-neutral treatment and deficient authorization of rivalry rules, in this way, prompting cross-sponsorship.

Also, to the degree that stage engineers set the standards of item and service development, just as in a commercial center connection, these influences get to, economic situations, and costs. Maybe the best estimation of stages comes from information removed nearly for nothing from clients. Taking into account that a large portion of this

Understanding Digitalization

advanced information is in some structure individual, they may not be treated as an item.

In e-commerce business, ceteris paribus, the negligible advantages for a common merchant partaking in a given stage, may diminish the higher the number of sellers. By contrast, the marginal benefits for stage designers may build, the higher the quantity of taking an interest merchants. Along these lines, while the main request advantages may have decreasing returns, the subsequent request advantages may have expanding returns, as proposed in Figure 2.

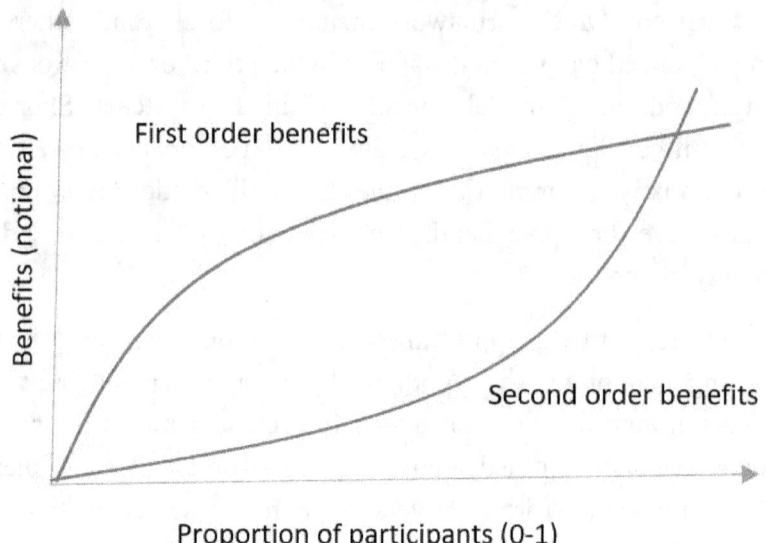

Proportion of participants (0-1)

The winner-takes-all dynamics joined with the system, and stage impacts along these lines, have enormous implications for rivalry. With information assortment and investigation progressively significant for the ascent of new services and arrangements, it is getting perpetually hard for a participant to challenge incumbents.

Enormous web-based business firms and stage engineers are consequently in a situation to catch a noteworthy and developing portion of the private advantages of digital commodities. This could be one of the clarifications behind the end of "unicorns," new companies worth about $1 billion that have been either crushed or acquired by the superstars.

Subsequently, we see a developing division in the worldwide economy between the individuals who use and the individuals who create, distribute, and manage digital technologies and set measures. The primary gathering is, to a great extent, made out of rising and developing nations, and even some high-salary economies that catch a portion of the principal request benefits. The second is generally made out of cutting-edge economies, for example, Germany, Japan, Sweden, the United States, and China.

By concentrating on first-request benefits and ignoring the essential significance of innovation improvement and the executives, numerous nations are giving up the chances of taking advantage of second-request benefits. These advantages, thus, are getting progressively focused among a gathering of economies that are home to the "digital commodity producer" firms.

Implications

Rising economies need to define approaches with the aggressive objective of receiving second-request rewards. Arrangements focused on upgrading investment in web-based business, for instance, can help a nation's long-haul intensity if there is a reasonable understanding that an extra effort will be expected to push the economy towards a place of digital innovation improvement.

Various activities should be mixed under a single national methodology planned for setting up the economy to go past the selection and utilization of such advancements. This isn't a simple errand, particularly in light of the fact that a portion of the arrangements intended to hold onto first-request advantages may not be lined up with arriving at second-request benefits.

Countries should seek a strong plan concentrated on information, one that works positively past framework and considers issues, for example, the age, stockpiling, preparing, and movement of information both inside and crosswise over national limits; information protection and security; tax assessment in the digital economy; and non-discrimination and access. This strong strategy plan ought to mirror the major changes that are happening in the types of creation; the significance of immaterial capital; innovation and marketing; and the generation of merchandise with worked-in services in an increasingly digital environment.

To feature the significance of this cross-cutting methodology, the system for digital improvement ought to have an advantageous association with strategies in the areas of trade, instruction, innovation, development, services, and rivalry. Trade policy, for instance, has progressively included components that go past conventional exchange, for example, administrations, internet business, information streams, protected innovation, and public procurement.

There is additionally a need to carry rivalry strategies to the advanced stage so they are capable of limiting oligopoly and monopoly positions and securing customer interests. If the advantages of the computerized economy generally gather innovation engineers and directors, there ought to be clear space for arrangement usage and guidelines. The coordination of these strategies at a high political level for consequent interpretation can decide the achievement of future projects intended to empower the development of platforms.

As we are managing new patterns, maverick nations should have the proactive, adaptable, and savvy type of commitment to figure out how to explore and determine benefits. To this end, policymakers should organize arrangements from the beginning, test, screen, assess, and collaborate.

Addressing digital divides is vital to empowering countries to receive and share the rewards of digital change. But, the asymmetric distribution of first- and second-request benefits inside and between nations can expand pay imbalance, in this way creating extra obstacles to the usage of the above strategies and the advancement of income convergence.

Understanding Digitalization

E-government is full electronic government, the utilization of data and communication technologies, especially the Internet, in government.

A famous method for conceptualizing e-government is to recognize three circles of innovatively interceded communications. Government-to-government connections are concerned about the utilization of advancements to improve the inner effectiveness of open organizations through, for instance, the automation of routine assignments and the fast sharing of data among divisions and offices. Government-to-business connections normally include the utilization of the Internet to reduce the expenses to the administration of purchasing and selling merchandise and services from firms. Government-to-resident collaborations include utilizing the Internet to give open services and transactions on the web and to improve the structure and delivery of services by fusing quick electronic criticism components, for example, surveys, Web overviews, and email.

Past this simple methodology, characterizing e-government is tougher; it is in a steady condition of development, and an enormous "gray literature" of white papers, interview records, consultancy reports, corporate handouts, and association tables has arisen. There are also unique national translations of the term; however, it crosses outskirts easily, making it arguably one of the quickest-spreading open-segment change thoughts ever.

Utilization of data and communication technology in government previously extended during the 1950s and 1960s, the prime of thoughts of logical organization. But e-government today is most normally understood as a plan for a general change of the open segments of liberal, law-based political frameworks. During the mid-1990s, US President Bill Clinton's organization drove this with the 1993 National Performance Review of the federal bureaucracy.

The explosion of Internet use in the mid-1990s offered stimulus to thought, and nations, for example, the United Kingdom, Canada, Australia, and New Zealand, followed with their very own variants. In the United Kingdom, the Labor Party chose in 1997 to put electronic help conveyance at the focal point of its program of modernizing government. In the same way, as different projects of hierarchical change, the cases made about e-government contrast considerably. They can be partitioned into two primary ways of thinking.

In one extensive viewpoint, the chief point is to utilize digital network technologies to open the state to a resident association. The ubiquity of PC systems offers the possibility of political investment to reshape the state into an open, intuitive system structure as an option, in contrast to both conventional, various-leveled, bureaucratic associations and later, market-like types of service delivery based on the contracting out of open area exercises (for the most part named the new open service).

Defenders of this point of view contend that far-reaching utilization of the Internet means that the customary use of data and correspondence advances in public bureaucracies, in light of internal confronting centralized server PC frameworks that began during the 1960s, should now be superseded by outward-facing systems in which the division between an association's inner data handling and its outer clients gets repetitive. The government turns into a learning association, ready to react to the necessities of residents, who are ready to impact public bureaucracies by fast, aggregative criticism instruments, for example, email, online discourse discussions, and intuitive Web locales.

A second, less extreme way of thinking recommends that e-government doesn't require more noteworthy open contribution in shaping how services are conveyed; however, rather by implication benefits residents through the proficiency gains and cost reserve funds delivered by the decrease of internal organizational friction primarily using the automation of routine assignments. Systems are additionally at the center of this viewpoint, yet a worry is about the capability of the Internet and intranets (inside authoritative PC systems) to join and facilitate the exercises of unique government divisions and services that are viewed as its most appealing component. In this view, residents are seen predominantly as the purchasers of public services, for example, medical services data, benefits installments, visa applications, government forms, etc. This has been the predominant model in those nations that have led the pack in presenting e-government changes.

E-government isn't without its critics. Some propose that changes are restricted to a managerial plan of service conveyance progressively steady with the new public management and that the open doors offered by the Internet for stimulating vote-based systems and citizenship may be missed. Different reactions are that the conservatism of existing managerial elites will scupper any possibilities of decisive change; that issues of inconsistent access (both inside and between states) to online services are being disregarded; that huge corporate data innovation interests are having an undue impact on the state of e-government; that conventional up close and personal contacts with local officials, particularly those related with welfare frameworks, can't be agreeably supplanted by Internet correspondence; that the cost investment funds guaranteed by changes have been hard to illustrate; and that bypassing of customary agent bodies (parliaments, committees) may happen, to the detriment of democracy.

Early government reactions to the Internet frequently went minimal more distant than putting data on the Web in a basic electronic adaptation of customary paper-based methods for scattering. The appearance of e-government, which flagged the acknowledgment of Internet availability as a device that could be utilized to improve proficiency, cut expenses, and change how governments have generally cooperated with residents, establishes a significant move in open organization.

To a few, e-government may appear to be little more than a push to extend the market of web-based business from business to government. Surely, there is some truth in this.

E-commerce is marketing and deals using the Internet. Since administrative foundations partake in promoting and deals exercises, both as purchasers and venders, it isn't conflicting to talk about e-government uses of online business. Governments do, after all, lead business.

But, web-based business isn't at the core of e-government. The center assignment of government is governance, the activity of managing society, not showcasing and deals. In the current majority rule, governments, obligation, and power for the guideline are split and shared among the authoritative, official, and legal parts of government. To some degree, the governing body is responsible for making strategy as laws, for actualizing the arrangement and law authorization, and for settling legal conflicts. E-government is tied in with improving these parts of government, not simply open organization in the limited sense.

New public management is a hypothesis about how to change government by replacing rigid hierarchical organizational structures with increasingly powerful systems of little authoritative units; replacing dictator, top-down choice and arrangement-making with a progressively consensual, base-up approach that encourages the interest of as many stakeholders as possible, particularly customary residents; embracing a more client-situated frame of mind to public services and applying market standards to upgrade efficiency.

E-government gives new public management fresh blood. Not exclusively does information and communications technology give the framework and programming instruments required for an coupled system of governmental units to work together successfully; the infiltration of this innovation into government organizations will in general lead normally to institutional change, since it is hard to keep up various-leveled channels of communication and control when each government employee can team up productively and legitimately with any other individual through the Internet.

Symmetrical to the division of intensity among the parts of government is the progressive association of supranational (e.g., European), national, provincial, and neighborhood governments limited by a topographical area. Information and communication technology makes another availability, conquering worldly, land, and authoritative limits. Accordingly, e-government can encourage new types of joint effort among governments that cut crosswise over and lessen such limits.

E-government isn't just or even essentially about changing the work forms inside and among governmental institutions. It is about improving its services to and joint effort with residents, the business and professional network, and not-for-profit and non-governmental associations, for example, affiliations, worker's guilds, ideological groups, places of worship, and public interest groups.

Utilizing World Wide Web portals to make one-stop shops is one well-known e-government way to deal with improving the delivery of public services to residents. The fundamental thought of these entryways is to give a single, convenient way to deal with every one of the means of a complex regulatory procedure, including different government workplaces, carrying the services of these workplaces to the resident as opposed to requiring the resident to run from office to office.

Web portals can convey taxpayer-supported organizations with different degrees of association. Three levels are normally recognized: data, correspondence, and exchanges. Data administrations convey government data using static site pages and pages produced from databases to residents, travelers, organizations, affiliations, open organizations, and other government clients. Communication services use groupware innovation, for example, email, discourse discussions, and talk to encourage exchange, support, and criticism in strategy-making methodologies. Transaction services utilize online structures, work processes, and installment frameworks to permit residents and colleagues to deal with their business with the government on the web. Common utilizations of exchange services for residents incorporate applying for social advantages, registering automobiles, recording changes of address, or applying for building licenses. For organizations, maybe the utilization of most noteworthy current interest is the online acquirement of government contracts.

Regularly, one reads that these three degrees of the association are requested by multifaceted nature, with exchanges being the most complex. Probably this is a direct result of the clear and testing security and business process reengineering issues of online transaction processing. Giving top-notch information and communication services is no less testing. Data services need to advance into information the executives benefit from and become adaptive, customized, proactive, and available from a more extensive assortment of gadgets. Communication services need to advance into coordinated effort services giving better help to argumentation, arrangement, consultation, and other objective coordinated types of organized talk.

Among the most fascinating socio-technological issues of e-government is in the region of eDemocracy, which expects to apply information and communication technology to improve the general supposition development process fundamental to the government's essential regulatory capacity. Here the desire is to expand real open interest, not simply the specialized probability, and counter political lack of care without disenfranchising the poor or poorly educated.

The following articles give a decent sign of the huge number and assortment of legislative procedures requiring explicit arrangements. Together with the pattern towards outsourcing tasks and working with industry in private-open organizations, this is probably going to prompt quick development of the e-government to advertise and make ample business openings for small- and medium-sized enterprises. The speculation is also planned for diminishing the size and expenses of government while quickening the development of the e-government market, making new organizations and occupations in the private sector.

The present residents anticipate that public services should be as customized and responsive as the services they get from the private area. Governments need to rethink how advancements can be utilized to improve the residents' understanding of public services. This requires the reception of a resident first culture and attitude in structuring arrangements and delivering services. The ultimate objective is to improve service quality, promote transparent and efficient interaction, upgrade the degree of open trust in government, and drive better resident results.

Social media and mobile platforms are replacing customary channels as a way to associate with government, report concerns, and give criticism. Mobile services, for example, applications and SMS, empower individuals to get to the services they need in a progressively helpful and focused way. These e-interest devices additionally empower more noteworthy coordinated effort with residents by including them in basic leadership, budget prioritization, critical thinking, and the co-design of services.

The utilization of cutting-edge examination enables governments to use information persistently accumulated from individuals and gadgets to improve service structure and personalize delivery. For instance, patients making web meetings with a health service provider could be guided to extra sources of help with their condition, for example, a nearby support group or exercise class.

Effectively, artificial intelligence (AI) can help convey services to residents, utilizing chatbots to finish exchanges inside government sites. It can help improve urban arranging by upgrading courses for transport services, reducing commuting time, giving instructive help to students dependent on their individual adapting needs, and empowering online self-referral and screening, signposting citizens to social services dependent on their needs and qualification.

Public Value

In an environment of uncertain growth and rising interest, governments must discover economical approaches to back public services and foundation. Digital technologies create chances to investigate new models for giving services, improve the use of assets through more astute spending, and connecting cash resources to projects and services based on the results they produce for residents, boosting responsibility and trust. Blockchain technology can help track how cash is spent through the framework, for instance, from money service to spending office and afterward, conveyance office. With better permeability of spending, governments can settle on better choices about how to allocate public resources.

Robotic process automation (RPA) offers speed and productivity, and the decrease of physically presented errors. A few governments are now utilizing a virtual workforce to robotize routine business forms, relieving the burden of high-volume, repetitive assignments, and saving time and assets that can be focused on frontline services.

Prescient investigation and content mining can make a significant commitment to the savvy executives of public resources by anticipating issues and empowering preventative activity, for instance, distinguishing citizens at risk of nonpayment.

Three-dimensional printing can improve turnaround time and lessen development costs for the framework and open transportation projects, build up increasingly proficient and lower-cost supply chains for resistance offices, and encourage work creation and monetary change of remote areas through the presentation of new assembling abilities.

Just as deploying these advancements to help growth, governments must think differently about their role, turning into a stage for a biological system of accomplices including offices, private organizations, not-for-profit associations, social enterprises, and citizens that together can create innovative services and plans of action.

Citizen Security

We live in questionable times. The threats from unpredictable states, terrorist groups, and other non-state entertainers is expanding and made progressively complex through digital technology. Today, clashes are waged in the combat zone as well as on public transport, on social media, and in cyberspace. Governments must protect their residents from an entire scope of threats, empowering them to live and work unafraid. Digitalization is both an obstruction and assistance in this battle.

From one perspective, as governments embrace digital technologies and become increasingly interconnected with partner associations and smart gadgets, new vulnerabilities emerge that can be exploited by cyber attackers. Terrorists, fraudsters, and hackers can jeopardize the conveyance of fundamental public services and the smooth running of common society, including the election process.

Then again, digital technologies and better information sharing give a modern method for battling dangers. Defense organizations are putting resources into AI, digital weapons and risk discovery programs, cybersecurity mechanical assembly, and advanced devices to make them nimbler and progressively viable. Police powers are utilizing versatile advances to lessen episode reaction times, while information examination is empowering prescient policing models and better risk investigation.

Residents are getting progressively worried about how their information is being utilized, so governments are acquainting data security the executives' frameworks with shield the information they keep and progressively depend on.

Economic growth, social cohesion, and equity of chance depend on a nation's workforce that is talented and prepared to grasp the necessities of the twenty-first century.

Governments need to assemble the abilities and capacities of their workers to drive more noteworthy efficiencies and reinforce assorted variety and incorporation. Governments need to accomplish more to pull in, hold, and create individuals with the necessary abilities and capacities. As they construct a progressively unique and responsive condition, governments will draw in more youthful specialists who are looking for jobs where they can have an effect on society.

Making this culture somewhat depends on governments allowing representatives an ideal opportunity to focus on all the more stimulating and value-adding tasks. This should be possible by sending insightful automation devices to supplement human specialists. Reducing the measure of manual and redundant work prompts more elevated levels of profitability and fulfillment, like the drawing in and holding qualified applicants and improving residents' involvement in taxpayer-driven organizations.

Mobile technologies can assist offices with enabling their workforce to carry out their responsibilities all the more adequately. As a great extent of open segment representatives consistently work outside the workplace, they can be outfitted with gadgets, for example, cell phones, tablets, and PCs, to play out their duties any place they're found.

While governments set up their very own workforces for the digital age, technological changes, for example, robotization and AI, have extensive ramifications for the fate of work, economics, and society as a rule. Governments must receive, refresh, and reinforce approaches to relieve antagonistic social and financial outcomes, for example, the relocation of laborers in some lower-gifted employments, and broadening social inequality.

Smart Infrastructure

A significant number of the present most essential difficulties urbanization, globalization, contamination, water shortages, and environmental change can be handled with shrewd foundation advancements, for example, connected cars, electric vehicles, smart power grids, energy-efficient buildings, Internet of Things (IoT) networks, and open data portals.

Governments are facing strong pressure to construct and redesign framework, especially in urban areas where the growing population is putting expanding pressure on maturing offices. Many developing nations need a new foundation to help their developing populations and expand financial movement while developing markets must reestablish a weakening or wasteful framework. The long period of underinvestment in the framework is presently making up for lost time in nations around the world. Assessments show that almost US$100 trillion all-inclusive should be spent on infrastructure in the following 20 years.

Smart infrastructure offers an approach to utilize the most recent advancements to get the greatest worth and effectiveness and make resilience and sustainability. It applies digital technology—for example, shrewd gadgets, sensors, and programming—to physical structures, from control plants to bridges. These canny gadgets empower progressively productive and viable observing and controlling of water frameworks, transportation systems, human services, and open security tasks, all central government capacities.

Governments should likewise seek arrangements to empower a flourishing digital economy. This includes working with private organizations to give improved 4G and approaching 5G systems and server farms, ensure high digital literacy among residents, advance digital incorporation, and empower secure access to services through advanced recognizable proof frameworks.

The open segment can't subsidize each framework venture itself; it must discover inventive methods for working with different financial specialists.

Risks in e-governance Systems

Any digitalized data faces threats from unapproved modifications during transmission through the Internet (hacking). Privacy, integrity, non-repudiation, and authentication (PINA) of information guarantees the effective working of e-governance. Without it, either dynamic hacking or detached hacking may occur. In detached hacking, the interloper listens to the data. In dynamic hacking, the interloper tunes in just as alter it as per the prerequisite, which at last violates the integrity of the data. To achieve Non-revocation highlight, the Information must be transmitted safely in such a way, that the genuine sender of the message neglects to deny its beginning. Confirmation of the data is built up just when the starting point of the message finishes the check assessment.

Modus Operandi of Attackers

In e-governance, information is powerless against dangers from the programmers and their corresponding attacks. As referenced before, these attacks can be either dynamic or detached. In both cases, an explicit calculation is pursued to break the security of the information. The modus operandi of the intruders can be seen as follows.

a. Overview and survey

b. Exploit and penetrate

c. Raise benefits

d. Maintain access

e. Prevent access

Right off the bat, the attacker plays out the review work to survey the attributes of the objective article. Having accumulated adequate data, the attacker attempts to abuse and infiltrate the application by finding the escape clauses of the system host and TCP/IP models. After the application is undermined, the attacker quickly endeavors to raise significant level benefits. Having picked up the entrance, the attacker steps up and keeps up the entrance in the future by covering their tracks. Indeed, even the assailants who can't access the framework mount attacks to avert the entrance of different clients.

The threat perceptions that endure during the e-governance exchanges can be arranged into the following.

Spoofing

In this method, the attacker attempts to pick up the entrance of the e-governance framework by utilizing deceptive personality either by stealth or by utilizing false IP addresses. When the entrance is picked up, the attacker abuses the e-governance framework by the rise of the benefits.

Tampering of E-Governance framework

When the framework is undermined and benefits are raised, the grouped data of the e-governance instrument turns out to be particularly powerless against unapproved modifications.

Repudiation

Indeed, the aggressor can mount a renouncement attack during the e-governance exchange, which is the capacity of the client to deny its performed exchange.

Exposure of E-Governance Information

If there should be an occurrence of the undermined e-governance framework, the unwanted information disclosure can take place very easily.

Denial of service

An attacker can perform a Denial of Service (DoS) attack by flooding the e-governance server with a request to expend the entirety of its assets to crash the instrument.

Elevation of privilege

When an e-governance framework is undermined, the attacker is claiming to be in a position of safety. The client endeavors to heighten the high profiles to get to its benefits to start further harm to the framework.

Cybercrimes

As a symptom of fast up-degrees of science and innovation, cybercrime rates have gotten higher, and it has affected the transactions achieved between the government and its citizenry inside the e-governance system. This threat can be characterized in the following classes.

False or malicious website

These sites are developed deliberately to take the citizen's significant data, like ID, secret phrase, credit, or credit card data. Bugs, for example, Freiburg Bug, spies on a guest's hard drive and transfers records from that point.

Theft of citizens' information from intermediary agents and ISPs

Residents may take the assistance of the Internet Service Providers (ISPs) and other transitional specialists while performing on the web money-related transactions like online expense installment, online ticket booking, and so on. Programmers may break into the frameworks of the specialists and ISPs to acquire the citizens' data.

Violation of citizens' privacy through the use of cookies

Cookies are a piece of data that a site moves on a client's framework hard drive for the upkeep of the account. The utilization of these to remove the data is also a threat to the protection of the citizens.

Spamming and flaming

Spamming is the indiscriminate sending of spontaneous email messages to Internet clients. Cybercriminals utilize this technique to spread PC infections to the frameworks of the citizen.

Like citizens, government offices likewise face risk from the attackers.

Citizen impersonation

In this method, the attacker claims to be a genuine citizen and executes the e-governance exchanges.

Ping of Death

Ping of Death is the method to send a huge number of information bundles to the e-governance cut off utilizing a ping order. Since the TCP/IP model will neglect to deal with that enormous measure of information, the server will be left with no different alternatives than to crash or reboot or hang.

Teardrop

The Teardrop attack abuses the defenselessness present in the reassembling of information bundles. During e-governance transactions, the information bundles sent over the Internet are separated into smaller parts and set up together at the goal framework. These packets have an offset field in their TCP header part which determines from which byte to which byte the specific information bundle is carrying the information. In the Teardrop attack, a progression of information parcels is sent to the objective e-governance server with covering counterbalance field esteems. Therefore, the objective framework neglects to reassemble the parcels and is compelled to crash, reboot, or hang.

Intranet-associated threats

An intranet is a system inside an association that uses Internet innovations to encourage information sharing inside the association. E-Governance offices may face threats from inside the association. Internal hackers are increasingly inconvenient because they have a potential abundance of data which they use in designing a malicious scheme.

The data transmitted on the Internet is broken into information bundles that may venture out over various courses to arrive at the goal. The most vulnerable purpose of interference of information is the purposes of the section to and exit from the Internet.

Risks associated with stored online E-Governance Information

Numerous E-Governance servers store data, which might be under the surveillance of intruders.

The risk associated with malicious code

The addition of malicious code, for example, infection, worms, and Trojan horses, can bring about e-governance server downtime. A virus is a malicious program that duplicates itself in some structure and performs unmentioned, numerous damaging acts. A worm contrasts from an infection in that it is a particular program that can run independently, though an infection program can't run without being embedded into another program. Trojan horse is another kind of noxious code that harms or destroys records. Trojan horses are unique from infections in that they don't imitate; rather, they sneak into the server by attacking a legitimate program. At the point when the influenced program is executed, the Trojan horse begins its destructive work.

The Advantages of Electronic-Government

A definitive objective of e-government is to have the option to offer an expanded arrangement of public services to residents in a productive and cost-effective manner. It takes into consideration government transparency, since it enables the general population to be educated about what the government is working on.

The favorable primary position while actualizing electronic government will be to improve the productivity of the present framework (paper-based framework). That would consequently save cash and time. The presentation would also encourage better interchanges among governments and organizations.

For instance, e-procurement encourages G2G and B2B correspondence; this will allow the smaller business to go after government contracts just as a larger business; thus, the upside of making an open market and a more grounded economy. Businesses and residents can acquire data at a quicker speed, any time of the day.

The general public is moving towards mobile connections, and the ability of an e-government service to be accessible to citizens regardless of the area, all through the nation, brings the following and conceivably greatest advantage of an e-government service as we live in what is presently named as the Knowledge time.

The anticipated advantages of e-government incorporate proficiency, improved services, better availability of public services, and more transparency and responsibility.

The Disadvantages of Electronic-Government

The fundamental disadvantage concerning e-government is the absence of correspondence apart from the web, unwavering quality of data on the web, and shrouded plans of government branches that could impact and bias public opinions.

Potential implications of actualizing and planning e-government incorporate disinter-intercession of the government and residents, impacts on monetary, social, and political elements, helplessness against cyberattacks, and aggravation to business as usual in these areas.

Hyper-surveillance: Once the administration starts to create and turns out to be increasingly refined, the residents will be compelled to associate electronically with the legislature on a bigger scale. This might prompt an absence of security for regular citizens as their service acquires increasingly more data on them.

Cost: Although a huge measure of cash is spent on the advancement and execution of e-government, the results and impacts of preliminary web-based governments are regularly hard to check or unsatisfactory.

Inaccessibility: An e-government webpage that gives online access frequently doesn't offer the possibility to include numerous individuals who live in remote areas, have low education levels, and exist on the poverty line.

What does e-Government Cover?

There are three primary spaces of e-government, delineated in Figure 1 (adjusted from Ntiro, S., 2000, e-Government in Eastern Africa, KPMG, Dar-es-Salaam):

- Improving government forms: e-administration
- Connecting residents: e-citizens and e-services
- Building outside cooperations: e-society

Understanding Digitalization

Individually, these especially address the issues that administration is excessively exorbitant, excessively wasteful, and excessively insufficient (e-administration), too self-serving, and excessively badly designed (e-residents and e-services); and excessively separate (e-society).

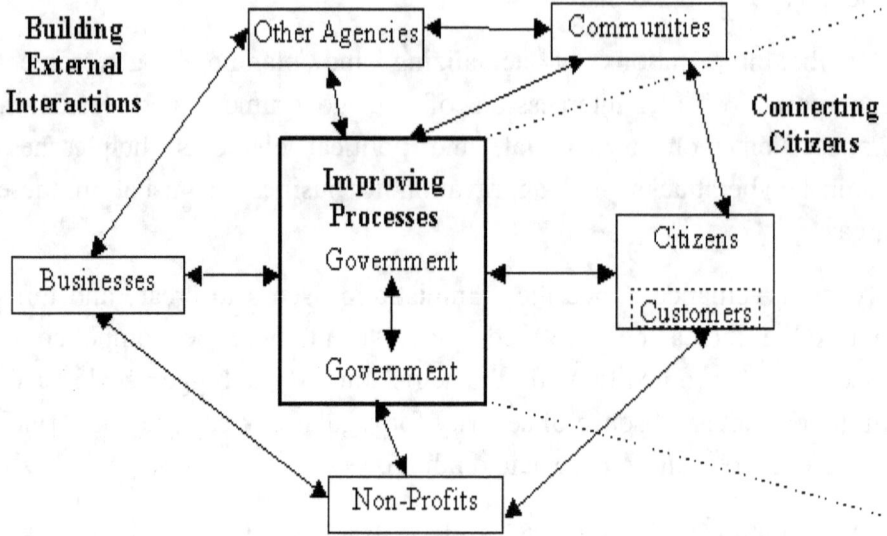

In somewhat more detail, the areas of e-government are as follows.

Improving Government Processes: e-Administration

E-Government activities inside this area manage to improve the interior operations of the open segment. They include:

- Cutting process costs: improving the input-output proportion by reducing monetary expenses or potentially time costs.

- Managing process performance: arranging, observing, and controlling the presentation of procedure assets (human, financial, and other).

- Making key associations in government: interfacing arms, organizations, levels, and information stores of government to fortify the ability to research, create, and actualize the methodology and strategy that aids government forms.

- Creating empowerment: moving force, authority, and assets for forms from their current locus to new areas.

Interfacing Citizens: e-Citizens and e-Services

Such activities manage the connection among government and residents: either as voters/partners from whom the open segment ought to determine its authenticity or as clients who expand public services. These activities may well fuse the procedure improvements distinguished earlier. They additionally incorporate a more extensive remit:

- Talking to citizens: giving citizens with details of open segment exercises. This mostly identifies with particular sorts of responsibility: making community workers increasingly responsible for their choices and activities.

- I am listening to citizens: expanding the contribution of citizens into open area choices and activities. This could be flagged as either democratization or cooperation.

- Improving public services: improving the administrations conveyed to individuals from the general population along with measurements, for example, quality, convenience, and cost.

Building External Interactions: e-Society

Such activities manage the connection between open offices and different foundations - other open offices, private segment organizations, and non-benefit and network associations. As with citizen connections, these activities may well fuse procedure upgrades. They additionally incorporate a more extensive transmit:

- Working better with business: improving the cooperation among government and business. This incorporates digitizing guidelines of procurement from and services to businesses to improve quality, comfort, and cost.

- Developing people group: building the social and financial limits and capital of nearby networks.

- Building associations: making authoritative groupings to accomplish monetary and social destinations. The open division is quite often one of the partners, however periodically it acts just as a facilitator for other people.

Chapter 8

Why digitization is important for your business

Digitization is a collective term. Initially, it is the way toward changing over data from the natural environment into a digital (computerized) group. This configuration presents information, which is spoken to as individual bits and gathered as bytes. It is also a term utilized for the transference of simple procedures into quicker, progressively efficient digital outputs.

The test in any digital improvement is to make an energizing, agile condition that draws in clients, conveys data to them quicker, whether in an office or on a production line. It is to limit the number of touch focuses and decrease preparation time.

Why is digitization so significant? It:

- improves the effectiveness of a business's procedures, consistency, and quality
- integrates records into a digitized system, removing redundancies and shortening the correspondences chain
- improves accessibility and encourages better data trade for staff and clients
- improves reaction time and client care anyplace on the planet
- reduces costs/working expenses

- provides an ability to exploit investigation and genuine client information

- helps with the adaptability of staff and diminished overheads

- improves plan for business coherence and development

Industries that have embraced digitization well

The PC games and film businesses are maybe the most evident instances of digitization and digital refinement, building exact and inventive situations to connect with, summon, and energize the client, and when time is money quick turnaround is essential.

Another carefully aggressive market is the online gambling club industry, a phenomenal case of how genuine Vegas-type conditions are shipped and digitized to bring the client an outwardly invigorating, energizing, and rewarding experience. Engagement is upgraded to keep clients on the site for whatever length of time conceivable to improve ongoing interaction, satisfaction, and faithfulness. This improvement in streamlined computerized forms is effectively recognizable in customer service, call determinations, texting, and significantly more. In such an aggressive market, client services are pivotal.

1. Try to exceed expectation. Don't move toward digitization indifferently; embrace it and attempt to push the breaking points of your digital condition. Make the upgrades that set aside your time and cash.

2. The more connections in the chain, the more shortcomings it presents during economic change.

3. Ensure that your digitization approach benefits staff and clients the same.

4. Consider utilizing programming to remove redundancies.

5. Operate the leanest and effective business you can within your spending limit.

Programming can improve information forms, which may have been finished by an individual from staff, profiting your business by saving additional time and disposing of the danger of human mistakes. Lots of popular technical expressions will be utilized to describe digitalization in guides and introductions, yet in truth, it is a basic procedure; it is tied in with helping organizations to help themselves in an all the more demanding digital era.

For more thoughts on the most proficient method to get your information online here is a valuable article by Laura Ziegler, marketing manager at Image Process Design, LLC. She clarifies how you can change your association's tasks with the cloud.

There is no uncertainty what so ever, that the cloud is upsetting both business and regular day to day existence. The buzz identifying with cloud includes its mechanical capacities, the advantages, helping organizations to work more astute, so the selection of cloud can have a digital transformation.

Today, organizations of every kind are beginning to utilize advanced innovation to sidestep the impediments of the physical world. New advances in this field enable them to discharge their items to the market quicker, to arrive at the correct clients, while offering a close to the right client experience. In spite of the fact that the world began digitization decades back, we are still just making child strides contrasted with what can be practiced later on.

In this article, we will assist you with posing the correct questions to decide whether you can utilize digital arrangements yourself to enable your organization to arrive at its maximum capacity.

There is a lot of motivations to begin digitizing your very own organization, and a blog entry wouldn't be sufficient to discuss everything here. For the time being, we gathered 7 normal reasons why you ought to consider introducing digital technologies with your business forms.

Understanding Digitalization

Toward the finish of each point, we will furnish you with certain inquiries that you can pose to yourself. Our objective here is to see whether it is the ideal opportunity for you to begin considering digitization as a genuine technique for developing your business.

Digitization is Significant for Your Business

1. Your industry is open for interruption

Regardless of which industry you are in, everybody is vulnerable to disturbance. On account of digital technologies, new or existing players can upset how individuals see an item or service, making what different organizations offer in that industry old. Would you like to be disturbed or become a disruptor? The decision is yours.

Uber is presumably the best and most utilized model for the disturbance. The organization utilized digitization perfectly to give a great client experience. They offer a quicker, less expensive, increasingly agreeable arrangement contrasted with taxi services.

If somebody finds a better approach to take care of your clients' issues, you need to react. One approach to keep your business from falling behind is to follow industry trends intently, buy into each divert that is picking up in fame, monitor what your clients, rivals, and accomplices are discussing. These channels can become brilliant wellsprings of new thoughts and approaches to enable your target market.

Another significant activity is to pay attention to each contender. A lot of market-driving organizations choose to dismiss newcomers instead of committing time and assets to truly become acquainted with their technique. History discloses to us that many of them wake up one day to understand that they have just fallen behind. Consider the thing individuals said about Twitter in 2006 and where the administration is at present.

Some significant questions to pose to yourself:

- Are you aware of competitors who are offering better approaches to answer client needs?

- Are you forward-thinking about the most up-to-date drifts in your industry?

- Do you have the chance to turn into a disruptor for your industry?

2. You have to improve ordinary productivity

Regardless of how productive you think you have become, there is consistently an opportunity to get better. Utilizing obsolete, inherited frameworks, working procedures physically that could be mechanized, poor correspondence among laborers and supervisors, and so on, mean that you are managing genuine issues that can be unraveled utilizing digital solutions.

You will find that work procedure digitization extraordinarily speeds up, particularly if the framework is fabricated explicitly around your business. Also, you can at long last change from the pen and paper configuration to the cloud, which is advantageous for both your business and the earth.

The way that you are now utilizing some software doesn't ensure the most productivity. The software continually needs to advance and adjust to new business conditions and scale together with the organization. On the off chance that your present software is moderate and questionable with visit crashes, or contrary to your more up-to-date frameworks, you likely need to think about updates or substitution. Replacing your inefficient software, as a rule, sets aside your cash in the long-term, contrasted with the significant expenses of keeping up obsolete frameworks.

Some significant questions to ask yourself:

- Do you have any manual work forms that could be automated?

Understanding Digitalization

- Is your present programming framework causing disappointments among your workers?

- Are your product support costs outpacing the worth it gives?

3. You must offer the best client experience

Perhaps you are not offering the correct client experience to your intended interest group. A quick and smooth client experience is basic to prevail available, as clients today are utilized to moment delight.

Pizza Hut can be a genuine model for new and inventive client experience arrangements. They realize that their clients despise waiting for their nourishment in cafés. They figured out how to battle weariness by making the whole requesting procedure intelligent utilizing contact screens.

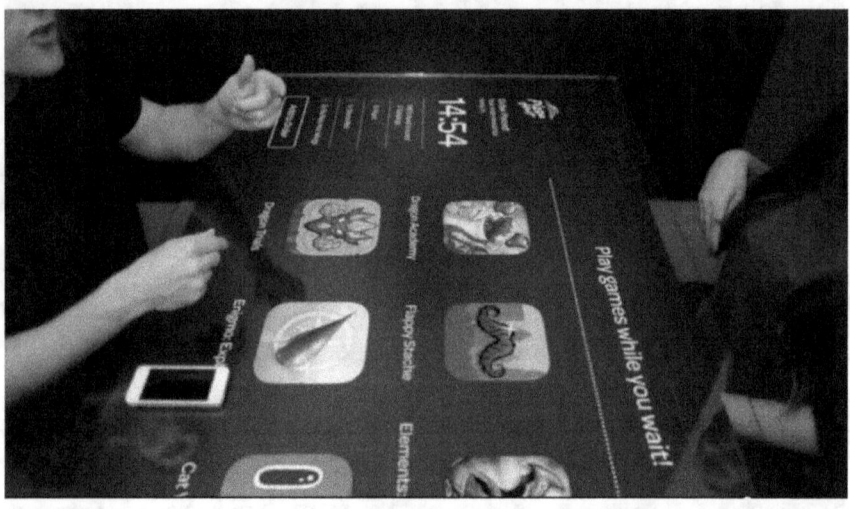

The bag is another organization that pre-owned digitization to locate an imaginative answer for probably the most seasoned issue: "Most men hate shopping."

They gather information about your taste inclinations on their site. At that point, their group assembles hand-picked outfits to meet your inclinations and sends them to your doorstep. In a couple of clicks, men can get a bag customized to their needs. If you don't like what you get, send it back altogether or in part for nothing. Along these lines, men can generally put their best self forward while never going out on the town to shop themselves.

Consider your very own business. Consider your clients' needs and regular issues, and attempt to discover new, inventive answers for them. You don't need to be a global mammoth to offer the best understanding; you simply need to break new ground.

Some significant questions to pose to yourself:

- Do your clients face any troubles while utilizing your item/service?
- Can you make your item/service simpler to access for your clients?
- Can you tap into new sources to gather feedback about your clients' needs?

4. Utilizing new channels to their maximum capacity

We need to stress the significance of information based on basic leadership with regards to online channels. Right utilization of information isolates effective online campaigns from simply throwing cash out the window.

Information from your internet-based life—pages, site, web shop, blog, and every other stage you are utilizing ought to be gathered, broken down, and considered while executing your online technique. Following transformations, commitment, site traffic, lead age, and other significant key performance indicators (KPIs) is fundamental to upgrading your online efforts.

Most organizations are not utilizing enormous information to their maximum capacity yet. It is hard to incorporate all the data from these different sources and see the full picture. For instance, each web-based life stage has an alternate interface, which makes it hard to analyze the data from each website.

Online life API coordination can give an answer to this issue. You can make a product arrangement that assembles all the information from your social pages and incorporates it in a solitary stage. Having everything in one spot can assist you with increasing a deeper insight into your clients' behavior and save a ton of time also. This is only one case of the unlimited ways digitization can assist you with getting more incentive out of your business information.

Some important questions to ask yourself:

- Do you realize what channels your intended interest groups are utilizing?

- Do you have a reasonable objective and methodology to contact your crowd?

- Can you use the information to enable your business to adjust to your clients' needs and habits?

5. Think about mobile users

If you start digitization without adjusting to mobile clients, you are certainly doing something incorrectly. Individuals are shopping, browsing, and associating on their telephones like never before, and the numbers continue developing. AdWords information additionally shows that about 70% of site guests found their site through their cell phones.

Regardless of whether you don't sell your services through cell phones legitimately, you should figure out how to draw in mobile users. Try not to spare a moment to build up an application that supplements your item. Take a look at what Nike has done. They sell sports hardware, yet made an application that keeps tabs on your development when you go out for a run.

In the healthcare industry, specialists, for the most part, have their hands full of individuals requesting consultancy, so they required electronic medical account (EMR) applications to turn out to be additionally time-productive. Designers delivered, and these applications currently make it workable for patients to track, screen, and share their information and ask questions through the application, ultimately saving the doctors' valuable time.

Somebody even made an application for ranchers to follow where their cows are, check if their livestock is healthy or when the cows are expected to be pregnant! The potential outcomes are unlimited. Be creative, discover arrangements, and build up your thought and added benefit.

If you do choose to upgrade your site for versatile clients or make your mobile application, ensure that the final item is exceptionally responsive, spotless, and simple to explore on each gadget.

Some important questions to ask yourself:

- Is my site adjusted and receptive to mobile clients?
- Can you praise your customary item/service with a mobile application?
- Can you use application and gamification to further your potential benefit?

6. Your production network

Digitization and new advances enable your business to make the worth chain shorter and offer more value to your clients. Today, organizations can take everything into their own hands, including distribution, promotion, and building brand awareness. You can purchase shoes directly from Nike, devices from Black and Decker, vehicles from Tesla, PCs from Apple, etc.

Today, everybody can set up their online retail channel without hardly lifting a finger. New players regularly start selling their items in their online stores and only open physical stores later when their image has picked up acknowledgment.

You don't need to be a globally recognized brand to make a fruitful deals channel for your items. Web-based business website designer stages like Shopify or Magento can assist you with beginning regardless of whether you have any web advancement or structure abilities. Once your web shop is prepared, you can get traffic by running an online advertisement with AdWords, Facebook, and Twitter ads, and so forth. You have each instrument you have to begin today readily available.

You can also bring marketing and advancement into your very own hands through content marketing. Locate the key interests and pain points of your intended interest group, make content that is useful, informative, or essentially a good time for them, and offer it through channels like a blog, online networking, or sites like Medium.

Some important questions to ask yourself:

- Can you make more of an incentive by bypassing the go-between?
- Can you utilize any online devices to fabricate your very own business and media channels?
- If you are the go-between, would you be able to turn into a media brand yourself?

7. Use innovations

Ignoring new technologies and solutions will make you fall behind to increasingly creative organizations. Artificial intelligence (AI), the Internet of Things (IoT), and large information are only a couple of models for advancements that can offer you new chances. Amazon is the ideal model here. They have huge amounts of data about their clients. They are currently utilizing AI to foresee shopper purchase behavior to reduce shipping time. Their definitive objective is to accomplish a one-hour delivery time for any request.

They also need to fuse large information innovation into their procedures to achieve this. Amazon, as of now, has a popular IoT item called Alexa. It goes about as your advanced partner that enables you to utilize voice directions to shop on the web, turn on different gadgets around the house, and significantly more.

You don't need to be a gigantic organization like Amazon to utilize these new advances. You can try different things with deals and marketing automation yourself with the assistance of AI and huge information. For instance, AI can assist you in utilizing all your gathered information about your clients.

For IoT, consider new answers to add advanced innovation to your current item in a manner that makes an extra incentive for your clients. Keen coolers that assist you with requesting food supplies, savvy shirts that can follow your pulse, shrewd cups that show drink temperature, and so forth. The conceivable outcomes are inestimable about IoT.

If you sell an item, ensure it is good with what's to come. Use the information to further your potential benefit, utilize digitization and AI to dissect everything that you can. Continue following trends and developments, and all the more critically, act now! Anybody can turn into the next big thing, so why waver?

The following is just a portion of the favorable circumstances that digitalization can offer you.

– Digital presence

This is likely the most obvious preferred position. The nearness on the Internet, through devices, online stores, informal communities, web journals, corporate pages, etc., increases the permeability of the organization and deals channels.

For certain organizations, this nearness is the focal point of their digital procedure, and they have even moved their business from conventional structures to online trade.

– New contact channels with clients

Similarly, the advanced nearness opens up deals channels and better approaches for speaking with clients. Email, applications, informal communities…these days, the customers of any business with a digital presence have different methods to contact the organization.

This is another approach to expand deals, reliability, and client loyalty; however, it also involves new obligations. Also, that is the reason giving support of all these new channels of correspondence requires doing things well.

– The client at the core of the universe

The digital transformation includes setting the client at the focal point of the business, and keeping in mind that this includes work and duty; it additionally offers significant advantages.

One of them is to discover their assessments. Contacts, for example, those built up in interpersonal organizations or opinion polls and websites, encourage the constantly significant errand of discovering users' opinions of items or services.

This closeness to the client infers obligation. The facts confirm that occasionally it will cost exertion and economic investment.

– Better basic leadership

Digitization goes inseparably with information, and information leads to better choices.

The digitalization of business makes it conceivable to have continuous contact with the client, and this enables us to become better acquainted with him/her. A few organizations go further and apply big data when settling on a wide range of choices that influence nearly the whole business (marketing, production process, etc.).

– It improves proficiency and profitability

This is probably what concerns you the most. Consider this. You have more data, which enables you to settle on better choices and mechanical tools to make your work simpler.

When utilized wisely, the digitalization of business can prompt a critical increment inefficiency and can reduce expenses. Innovation has helped organizations to improve in these areas consistently. Digitalization can also do this.

– It encourages innovation

The digital transformation drives us to act. What's more, when the development starts, the inertia will make it harder to stop.

The digitalization of business, for the most part, prompts a dynamic of innovation that enables it to be increasingly mindful of new patterns and the potential outcomes offered by innovations. Also, it can help cultivate advancement among colleagues (if they are permitted to utilize it). Innovation won't just rely upon digitalization, however, it will also accomplish more.

– It makes communication and teamwork easier

Both through the arrangement of objectives and the opening of new communication channels, the digitalization of business improves inside communication. We can watch this both through the collaboration (for example, between departments) that will be expected to actualize proportions of digital change and through such essential decisions as executing an inside talk. Recollect this is the motivation behind why they call the present the age of communication.

– It improves working conditions

The potential outcomes that digitalization offers in an organization spread across numerous areas, and one of them is the improvement of working conditions. New business choices, for example, adaptable working hours or teleworking, need the help of digitalization. Without this, it would be substantially more difficult or even impossible.

And, improving working conditions offers different advantages, for representatives, yet additionally for the organization. It assists a decline in job turnover and increment ability maintenance. The new ages of laborers (the purported twenty- to thirty-year-olds) request digitalization in their occupations. If it is not offered, there will likely be significantly less interest.

The digitalization of business isn't constantly a basic procedure, yet it can bring extraordinary advantages. What's more, the market powers this, and the organization that neglects to do so will presumably have issues in keeping up its intensity.

Since we've seen a portion of the advantages of an organization's computerized change, what about taking a couple of moments to find out about eHorus?[xx]

EHorus is a remote PC (remote work area programming) that could assist you with certain parts of the digital change in your business.

The expanding venture by organizations in digital activities is directed by the clients who expect services and items conveyed to be quick and efficient. Acing digitalization is tied in with setting up a refreshed layer for future new tech applications for making the existence of the venture progressively streamlined and presenting a new nature of client experience.

In the battle to effectively grasp advanced patterns, organizations move their items and services into the digital environment and assemble new plans of action altogether not to be deserted. For instance, advanced trendsetters like PayPal, Uber, and Airbnb acknowledge ordinary cordiality, monetary, retail, and transport enterprises in an extraordinary way. Also, they demonstrate to be effective.

Organizations that don't get acclimated with change before long will become obsolete.

Ongoing CEB examines that:

Digitizing your business conveys different advantages, like decreased costs, expanded security, and improved efficiency. Among the entire vectors of computerized change, we'll address two parts of the digital condition: information and mobility.

In a data-driven world, it's the information we remember when thinking about digital trends. Making your information advanced encourages you to create a superior business.

Initially, you save money on expenses and time. Records in a digital position put away in the cloud streamline your costs—less office space, fewer organizers, less paper, fewer assets to work on them physically. Printing, arranging, and recording requires huge amounts of billable working hours rather than a couple of clicks of a mouse.

Also, you get improved performance and efficiency. With all the basic business information accessible continuously on a cell phone, you and your representatives get to it whenever, from, for all intents and purposes, all over the place, beginning from far-reaching money-related data on stock statements, advertising information, communication with clients in a proficient route, and up to handling laborers ready to convey every one of the progressions immediately.

Generation C

The hyper-associated digital biological system produced the requirement for organizations to offer elite and personalized services for their customers.

Generation C ("Connected") want to collaborate with specialist co-ops using cell phones and won't invest energy nor endeavors for physical presence in a bank to make an exchange, book a trip at the carrier's organization office, or drive to a café to make a table reservation. Today we would prefer to appreciate the consistency and nonstop accessibility from the suppliers taking a gander at the screen utilizing the entire abilities of cell phones.

The world readily available

An overwhelming, all-presence of cell phones advanced into everyday life. According to Statista, the vast majority of the information, web included, is gotten to by utilizing a cell phone and remote gadgets: communication, online life, business forms, following wellbeing, gaming, and security surveillance.

Organizations think of portability as a distinct advantage in each kind of service. To get it right, versatile applications are currently the essential driver to draw nearer to a client.

The power of apps

The power of apps is difficult to belittle. Created and specially crafted applications matched with explicit highlights and ease of use have demonstrated to contain a colossal promoting power. Rich usefulness, beginning from consistent online installments and requesting to gamification and diversion components are powerful enough for buyers to help out their preferred image every day.

Organizations experience great profit by the progressing commitment, since faithful clients utilizing their application make normal purchases, orders, and recommend the organization to their associates. Versatile applications can be a genuine element of bringing business advertising and deals advancement procedure to the next quality level.

Technology evolvement makes it significantly simpler today to create and dispatch an application for business and furnish it with target-explicit usefulness. This speculation truly pays off as organizations spare time and expenses for order prep and satisfaction, accepting crucial information, and fitting in with clients' requests by the day's end.

Center points of interest of a mobile application for your organization:

- No geolocation limits. Your services get a worldwide reach; they can be gotten to and prepared anyplace, independent of area. An application is a significant instrument to stretch out your contributions to any Internet client, regardless of the nation or the continent.

- Added esteem for your clients. Robust apps with upgraded ease of use assist with timing and endeavors on handling, submitting, criticism, and bits of knowledge sharing.

- Marketing in a hurry. A custom application publicizes and promotes your items or services in a viable, opportune way when a client downloads or launches it. Your marketing technique, effectively translated using current portability devices, can help focus on your clients and improve advertising reach.

- Increased deals. A responsive application helps clients to immediately use offered services whenever and from nearly anyplace on the planet. They are an immediate channel to associate with the clients and encourage them to purchase your items or services.

- Brand awareness. Drawing in clients with your marked application is the opportunity to develop business with brand awareness. Standard collaborations and customized contributions make clients increasingly steadfast.

- Information sharing. Well-custom-made applications give both general data about an item or service and present new advancements as a type of direct connection with clients.

- Social engagement. Mobile applications are the drivers of public activity, regardless of if one prefers the idea or not. They empower clients to mingle, watch the news and updates intently, to like, offer, and remark on items and services through installed internet-based life catches. This isn't just a method for communication, but a feasible deals driver for the suppliers.

Types of applications for businesses

There are countless business-situated applications. They can be characterized by their motivation. Here are some fundamental kinds of utilizations.

1. Loyalty applications

These work as a predictable component of offers over channels and upgrade communication by expanding client spending. Dependability frameworks as an idea empower helpful administration of the entire assortment of extraordinary ideas for a particular target audience. These applications gather enormous volumes of pertinent client information, including demography or land information. They additionally involve client standards of behavioral patterns, interests, and purchasing inclinations.

2. Office productivity apps

These are the applications keeping up nonstop office execution data. A few organizations practice the utilization of gamification components inside their applications for better motivation and inspiration for the workers. The general reason for workplace profitability applications is to expand the business profitability, commitment, and productive execution of the representatives.

3. Mobile CRM and sales support apps

Mobile CRM (client relationship management) applications are increasing greater notoriety in the hyper-connected society. It gathers client data in a database over various channels, gathers the status of requests, tracks history of purchases and connections (past and arranged), client care issues, preferences and sentiments, and most significant, they give continuous examination, detailing with the dispatch of AI. This makes a significant information pool for deals, client commitment, and promoting staff to give better client involvement with all purposes of the client lifecycle, optimizing marketing efforts, automating work processes, and tracking execution and increment incomes.

4. Business-explicit apps

This is most likely the greatest classification that incorporates the business-situated applications intended for specific business needs. Be it an application for a voyaging organization or protection supplier, they all are advancing the administrations and contributions of a specific organization to their clients. By and large, those are exceptionally assembled applications with flawlessly planned convenience and essential usefulness, instant communication with the supplier and are arranged on a variety of the suppliers' administrations.

5. Appointment scheduling apps

Booking applications are the need for some clients these days. They help with the management of internet booking and appointments, and regularly incorporate online payment options. These incorporate various crucially significant highlights, like programmed dashboarding, booking confirmation, accessibility estimation, reminders, etc., that help to keep in contact and order. In many cases, they are synchronized

Understanding Digitalization

with the third party applications, which makes it truly agreeable for a client to control everything over all gadgets.

Chapter 9

Challenges with Digitization

Challenge 1: Data Management:

Controllers must make clear that the management of information is a higher priority now than at any time in recent memory. An essential for the important utilization of a lot of digital information, for example, with prescient examination or worth driver trees, are fine-grained, mistake-free crude, and ace information. If these are not accessible, any fancy tools and coming about digital renderings will be of little worth ("trash in, trash out"). In like manner, in the digital age, the generally much-despised administration of crude information assumes a considerably more noteworthy job. An extra—and no less significant—task of controlling is to guarantee the consistency and similarity of different information and investigation models inside the organization. This duty is likewise still regularly neglected.

Who has the lead? From the controlling perspective, the appropriate response is basic: Controllers must guarantee that sway over the management of money-related and non-financial raw and master information lies in the controlling division. Today, the business office is regularly still accountable for client-related information, while workforce information has a place with HR, and so on. Such practices look bad in the digital age.

Controllers should likewise characterize their job in connection to the recently rising information science focuses, where mathematicians, physicists, and PC researchers investigate organized and, particularly, unstructured information (masses) from every single applicable area of the worth creation chain. If controlling means to remain the "single purpose of truth" inside the organization, this has extensive results, particularly concerning the association of informing the board.

Challenge 2: Self-Controlling

Controllers must lead the democratization of data to get to and empower directors to transform the thought behind the main idea energetically. Three essential IT patterns will help them en route: self-service, mobile information access, and continuous information. Accordingly, managers can access information, to a great extent, free of controllers. Simultaneously, applications standardize analyses to a more noteworthy degree than before. At the point when esteem driver trees are additionally furnished with an appealing and intelligent front-end (for example, SAP's digital meeting room, cf. Weber 2016), this infers not just democratization of data. Or maybe, the fundamental rationale of driver trees can also be incorporated into decision-makers' discussions.

Controllers can never again depend on their built-up job as watchmen. Simultaneously, simple examinations will never again be seen as a worthy commitment from controlling when they are exceptionally institutionalized and can be led without a controller's help. As for setting originators, controllers can keep on producing extensive worth. Specifically, it is imperative to screen the level of self-administration and constant in an organization and guarantee ideal degrees of both.

Challenge 3: Agile Control

The executive's control forms must become leaner, better incorporated, and quicker—in short, progressively dexterous. The implications of digitalization work out in a good way past the democratization of data arrangement. To effectively deal with a digitized worth chain, the board must get slimmer, better coordinated, and quicker. Indeed, even today, the prescient investigation can be utilized to create robotized estimates from granular information, which are regularly more solid than conventional gauging strategies.

Simultaneously, the related mechanization of a huge segment of the determining procedure guarantees significant efficiency gains. At long last, robotized figures, together with pre-characterized choice parameters, can, in this way, be utilized for the digital cost and amount alterations, for instance, in retail.

Digitalization will change the regular time allotment of the executive's control forms. Fast activity over the year is getting progressively significant, though the recurrence of criticism circles is developing. Along these lines, yearly control cycles will lose significance. Simultaneously, controllers must figure out how to manage vital (and operational) vulnerability. At the point when setting up plans of action are progressively addressed and advanced options bring about the furious challenge, vulnerability increments, the consistency of the business in this way decreases.

Challenge 4: Efficiency in Controlling

Digitalization must be deliberate in expanding productivity in the controlling office. From one viewpoint, digitalization involves an interest in lean, incorporated, and responsive control. Then again, the previously mentioned potential for robotization, just as with the worldwide institutionalization and centralization of controlling procedures, make huge effectiveness gains in account conceivable. Because of both firmly related improvements, a significant bit of the conventional "unburdening" assignments held by controllers will be disposed of. Thus, as it is regularly claimed, controllers would then be able to concentrate on progressively significant assignments.

As a general rule, however, proficiency gains normally are and will keep on being accomplished using shared assistance focuses, which were created given that accurate objective.

Challenge 5: Business Partnering

As a colleague, the controller must help the organization's digital change with productive analysis. A few perspectives can be recognized.

In the digital change intermingling stage, the controlling office must inspect the overall allotment of assets to advanced versus simple business areas and, if necessary, request changes. It's anything but a simple exercise in careful control. It's important to drive the digital change energetically while all the while keeping up sufficiently high short-term profitability.

It is essential to keep unwanted management exercises from interfering with the change procedure. In this unique circumstance, the best possible distribution of digital incomes and change-accommodating motivations for the customary association are only two significant focuses that controllers must address.

Simultaneously, a principal social change must happen. If an organization is to be effective in a setting of high vulnerability and digital change, a corporate culture of open data trade and helpful analysis must win and, if vital, supplant politically propelled trades and a progressive storehouse mind-set. Device and procedure-based arrangements might be fundamental and supportive; be that as it may, the focal driver in managing instability (cf. Schäffer/Weber 2015b) and digital change is an organizational culture that empowers basic talk and the open trade of data. Controllers, specifically, must set a genuine model.

Challenge 6: Analytics

Controllers must reinforce the investigative capability of their organizations. If controllers are to be paid attention to as a colleague in an advanced setting, they should not be restricted to little information. Controllers should also build up their competency profile in measurements and data innovation.

Understanding Digitalization

As to the new experts known as data scientists, essential hierarchical inquiries emerge: Are information science focuses some portion of controlling or IT? Is huge information broken down in a focal unit or decentralized in a provincial organization? How do smaller organizations manage the issue? Our impression: Controllers have to date, to a great extent, neglected to address this inquiry. Generally speaking, they see large information as a promoting and inventory network point. The suggestions for the executive's control forms are seen uniquely to a restricted degree. In this way, the present talk is fulfilled when controllers and information researchers (only) agree when cooperating: Controllers don't need to ace every single factual technique in detail. Despite what might be expected, it is adequate to pose the correct inquiries, have adequate diagram information, and ace the language of the information researchers. However, if this works out as intended: What worth do controllers still contribute? What keeps managers from turning directly to the data scientists?

Challenge 7: New Skills

Controllers should additionally build up their fitness profile. The job of a colleague in an undeniably digital setting requires various significant abilities. Moreover, ease when working with numbers and the conventional necessities for efficient and methodological capabilities, the information in measurements and data innovation, social and relational abilities, and a strong comprehension of the business are developing in significance (cf. Gänßlen et al. 2013). The necessities for the fitness profile of controllers keeps on developing.

Challenge 8: Controlling Mind-set

Controllers must question their very own idea designs. Today, controllers commonly center on effectiveness and gainful development. The issue is that the related choice and control rationale performs magnificently in nearly stable circumstances yet doesn't adapt well to disruptive changes, along these lines is digital change. The auspicious production of essentials for acing the digital future isn't supported.

Specifically, when controllers carry out their responsibility well, they chance not completely tending to the digital difficulties. Following Clayton Christensen, we talk about the controller's issue amid digital change.

Thus, controllers must figure out how to manage key (and operational) vulnerability. In this regard, the previously mentioned instruments can be useful. It is essential to change from speculation in parts of the year to evaluating ventures, from singular measures to portfolio points of view, and from safety-mindedness to an experimentation culture. For most controllers, this is genuinely not a simple step.

As digitization is being embraced by organizations, networks, urban communities, and associations large and small, it is basic to survey and address the difficulties that exist. Difficulties that can become gems for the Internet of Things (IoT); challenges that could decrease the guarantee of huge information; challenges that may push promising developments in areas of artificial intelligence, virtual reality, or biotech considerably further into what's to come.

Difficulties that can become huge business openings when tended to in a composed and legitimate manner. The rundown of difficulties to digitization below is in no way, shape, or form total, however, it addresses the most significant ones and how Cisco looks to address some of them.

The Art of Connecting Everything

With the exponential development of IoT and digitization, interfacing everything, safely and flawlessly, has become a genuine art. What is required is for the business to empower designs that take into account intermingling of a developing cluster of access advancements, end gadgets, sensors, programming layers, examination, and answers for meet up. Cisco drives the world in this space. Having said that, such structures require coordinated effort and understanding among partners in a booming ecosystem to become a reality.

Standards

The improvement of IoT has experienced an absence of gauges in the market. Exclusive conventions and divided markets demonstrated the standard as opposed to the special case. Without norms, IoT can't develop. Long stretches of progress and an enunciation point were seen in 2015 and 2016. While on the shopper's advertising side, the development of benchmarks is still in its beginning times, on the mechanical side, in areas such as road digitization or new advancements, for example, LoRa, principles rise, and certain conventions become true models. A ton of work needs to be done, and endeavors in the market to "self-standardize" are conveying a colossal lift to the general improvement of IoT.

Big Data

Big data has frequently been classified as "the new oil." Harvesting and utilizing enormous information is turning out to be standard, yet a lot of issues remain, particularly in the open space, with issues concerning possession, protection, and digital security. Who watches the information and guards the guardian? Neither the private part nor the administration can be exclusively trusted to give the full coordination of the administration of protection sensitive information. Satisfactorily tending to this test is one of the most significant authoritative issues of our day and age.

Security

Cybersecurity is at the forefront of everyone's thoughts regarding digitization. The world right now manages 2.5 million digital security risks each second. Justifiably, 60% of business pioneers are hesitant to improve due to digital dangers. Digital security is a huge test, but then added an extraordinary chance. Cisco sees it that way and has gotten one of the world chiefs in cybersecurity. No other association knows better where every parcel of information is sitting, where it's coming from and going to, and whether it should be there. Cisco conveys security in the system instead of including an answer on top of it. Cisco Talos[xxi] screens 600 billion messages each day. By and large, the identification of a typical rupture takes the influenced association 100 to 200 days to find. Cisco does it in 17.5 hours.

Skills and Jobs

In Europe alone, it is expected that 1.2 million IT-related occupation opportunities will exist in 2020. It is a test; this additionally makes a chance for colleges, specialized schools, governments, and the tech business. Cisco's Network Academy continually selects a huge number of experts around the world. The system's foundation has additionally become a significant part of the Country Digitization Acceleration activities Cisco has propelled in association with the legislatures of nations, for example, France, Germany, Italy, Mexico, and India.

Proof of Value

All digitization endeavors have innovation at their center. What drives the reception of these endeavors isn't such a great amount of confirmation of idea, but proof of value. Numerous IoT arrangements wind up at a phase where worth is being demonstrated in monetary, social, and natural terms. Building the proper business models isn't only a test; it is an open door for some in the market, and it is going on at a quick pace.

Understanding and Anticipating Impact

Digitization is setting off a monetary transformation. In the expression of Jeremy Rifkin, acclaimed thought pioneer: "The Internet of Things is the primary universally useful innovation stage in history that can take huge pieces of the economy to approach zero marginal expenses."

Take the vehicle industry in the US, for instance. Robotized vehicles will cause a significant effect on perhaps the greatest calling in the US inside 10 years: the activity of a driver. According to of Robin Chase, organizer of Zip Car: "There are 3.5 million cargo and conveyance truck drivers in the United States. There are 665,000 transport drivers. In New York City alone, there are 90,000 enlisted taxi drivers not tallying Uber and Lyft drivers. There are 5.5 million individuals assembling and planning autos and 1.65 million individuals working at dealerships. These occupations are at high hazard." The government and private sector should work together to anticipate and react to the exponential change digitization produces.

Why organizations battle to develop digital strategies

Organizations developing digital strategies are attempting to encourage changes because most CIOs are essentially not prepared to be digital leaders. While venture CIOs can make utilitarian innovation frameworks, many come up short on the visionary aptitudes required to be a change operator in the advanced age, as indicated by Shawn Banerji, overseeing accomplice of the innovation, digital, and information leaders practice at Caldwell Partners.

"CIOs who have that [enterprise operations] direction and range of abilities much of the time essentially don't have the vision and specialized inclination by a digital toolbox. For some associations, advanced was not the basic command that it is today, and the CIO's job mirrored a form and worked the useful utility mentality," says Banerji.

To get a handle on why organizations are enduring such a computerized shortage now, Banerji says you should look to some fundamental patterns. Before the 1990s and mid-2000s, most venture programming was uniquely worked by the organizations devouring it. That started to change when stirred by fears of shutdowns activated by Y2K; most Fortune 1000 organizations inked innovation redistributing contracts with residential specialist organizations, including EDS, ACS, and Perot Systems, just as abroad merchants, for example, Tata, Wipro, and Infosys.

Benefiting from these feelings of trepidation, Microsoft, Oracle, SAP, IBM, and a few other driving sellers landed large agreements to manufacture these undertakings. At the point when enterprises expected to redesign their innovation, their IT offices delivered the particulars to their partners, who built and implemented it.

With organizations selecting to offload their innovation abilities, a large number of their key IT laborers rushed to sellers and outsourcers, making a vacuum that Banerji says frequents undertaking IT divisions right up to today. This is a central motivation behind why such a large number of huge associations are enduring as digital laggards. "They lost that product designing capacity and the related IP," Banerji says. "Had those arranged individuals, stayed in their associations, one would peril that a least a couple would have climbed the authority pecking order and been organic catalysts of innovation. When they were gone, the transcendent purchase or rent vs. fabricate a bespoke system of the previous 15 years implied that most F1000 organizations were not employing and building up that ability and the associated software mindset dissipated."

Technology leaders who remained became uber program administrators and operational CIOs. While Banerji says these CIOs are "fantastic leaders with magnificent communication and partnership skills," most are, to a great extent, request takers as opposed to visionary pioneers fit for executing digital changes. And, that was fine—until it wasn't. Over the past few years, a significant number of these driving organizations have wound up upset by organizations, for example, Amazon.com, Uber, and Airbnb, whose computerized stages have produced tremendous system impacts. "In a generally packed time period, a large group of organizations, the greater part of the cloud locals, have developed and disturbed the norm, which will continue," Banerji says. "The goal lines have proceeded onward CIOs incredibly, rapidly."

How CIOs can drive change

Banerji prescribes heritage organizations embrace an innovative mind-set and muster the courage to roll out discount improvements. "Corporate leaders must have the humility and vision to see a future past the estimation of their inheritance tasks and distinguish approaches to bring development into their associations, regardless of whether it implies self-interruption. There are huge stores of undiscovered development in inheritance organizations simply trusting that the correct initiative will open it," Banerji wrote in another Caldwell report.

Banerji says that CIOs would do well to take a page from the playbook of organizations, for example, Amazon.com, whose CEO Jeff Bezos practices a Day 1 way of thinking that stresses concentrating on business results over procedures. The thought is to make high-speed, top-notch choices without getting bogged down in process while remaining laser-concentrated on clients. Only one out of every odd business is organized to rehearse the Day 1 way of thinking; however, a lot of conventional organizations are fashioning their very own digital playbooks.

Perceiving that its product can yield upper hands, Goldman Sachs made an API-based stage technique and publicly released such vital programming as its Securities Database, which processes more than 20 billion costs for each day on a huge number of positions the bank holds in stocks and different protections.

General Electric has done a computerized business with an expressed objective of turning into a $20-billion venture throughout the following few years. Domino's Pizza, perceiving the way Amazon.com and other internet business players were steamrolling retail, made an online pizza tracker as its initial step to turning into a computerized business. It's additionally exploring different avenues regarding voice acknowledgment innovation and mobile software.

CIOs are considering such moves and acting with recently discovered desperation. At the Forbes CIO Summit a month ago, numerous CIOs talked about dumping the moderate/quick crossover model of bimodal IT for essentially quick models to achieve digital velocity.

Chapter 10

Case studies

Digital Transformation Success Stories

Organizations are progressively propelling activities to extend or construct digital capacities that convey business productivity or top-line income development. However, the progress of digital changes fluctuates.

Thirty-five percent of 3,810 senior leaders as of late interviewed by Telstra have put more than $1 million in digital change items and services over the previous year, while 16 percent spent more than $5 million. Thirty-three percent of these leaders expect their all-out spend on a digital change to increase by more than 10 percent in the following three years, as per Telstra.

With organizations, for example, General Electric and others, stubbing their toes en route, numerous endeavors are trading wholesale transformations in favor of smaller, more measured innovation. Enterprises, it appears, are narrowing their openings for change, Forrester says. For instance, just 34 percent of banks and back up plans are changing promoting, and just 45 percent are changing client care.

"There is some fatigue around enormous brush digital change, and there is a requirement for tech leaders and e-business pioneers to make it littler," says Forrester Research investigator Allen Bonde. "Officials are currently saying, 'We get it—we will be disturbed, yet what would we be able to achieve rapidly or all the more for all intents and purposes?'"

Here, CIO.com offers a few previews of exceptions that are considering achievement to be they grasp advanced, in a perfect world to support business tasks or incomes.

WW

WW, the weight reduction and nourishment organization once known as Weight Watchers, has made the change to coordinated programming improvement and the cloud with an end goal to dispatch increasingly digital items. The organization, which has around 4,000,000 individuals, is putting resources into digital abilities to suit a scope of inclinations for managing health as a component of a continuous exertion to expand the brand impression past its in-person workshops, where customers get nourishment guidance.

In March, WW propelled Wellow,[xxii] an application that empowers clients to discover plans and calorie data and oversee weight reduction objectives through voice directions on Amazon Alexa and the Google Assistant stages, says Nic Chikhani, WW's VP. To benefit from the developing sense that shoppers like to utilize voice abilities at home, the organization will add capacities to Wellow to help walk clients through setting up a formula. Chikhani says the application is coordinated with WW's primary mobile application to give an extensive multi-channel understanding for purchasers. Chikhani selected to offer Wellow as a different application from the WW mobile application so as not to confuse clients.

Voice-oriented virtual assistants have a mixed reputation, to a great extent, because of the failure of brands to elevate them to clients, just as the general absence of comprehension of voice as a UI. Chikhani wants to change that with Wellow. "We are always emphasizing on the digital understanding," Chikhani says. "We need to meet individuals where they are."

Atlassian

Enterprise software creator Atlassian procured Archana Rao from Veritas Technologies to help make an innovation establishment to help the organization's next development spurt, including acquisitions. "The No. 1 need for the CIO job was scale," Rao says.

Not long after Rao joined, Atlassian gained OpsGenie,[xxiii] which required Rao to make procedures to help everything from onboarding OpsGenie representatives to coordinating procurement, deals, and different tasks.

Rao also re-platformed on a microservices engineering, running in AWS, while directing the organization's day of work to a SaaS membership-based charging model. Rao compared these parallel errands to "energizing the plane while it's noticeable all around."

The way to guaranteeing an effective M&A methodology? Making repeatable procedures, or a playbook for the procedures used to obtain new organizations. "It's worked for us as we move to the cloud," she says. "For IT, the No. 1 technique is to empower the business to scale."

In 2019, Rao is hoping to embrace mechanical procedure automation to automate repetitive tasks, for example, information passage in budgetary services, IT support, HR even assignments identified with the treatment of information under Europe's GDPR. She's also reflecting on the most proficient method to find bits of business knowledge and how to use artificial intelligence and machine learning.

StubHub

At the point when CIO Marty Boos joined StubHub seven years ago, the ticket retailer's foundation was battling to deal with the volume of a business that procedures a huge number of ticket exchanges daily for shows and games. To do as such, Boos manufactured a private cloud that scales flexibly, and to help worldwide transactions in the wake of StubHub's acquisition of Ticket is, Boos chose Google Cloud Platform to process payments locally in 44 nations around the world. "We're going to utilize that to get the exchange nearer to the buyer," says Boos, who has also grasped robotization capacities.

The cloud bolsters a few client-facing activities. With more than 50 percent of StubHub's traffic coming in from cell phones, StubHub is empowering dealers to utilize their telephone to click a photo of tickets and post them on the web.

The organization, as of late, included vivid 3-D capacities into its mobile iOS application to give buyers a superior idea of what they're purchasing. Customers can pinch and zoom to evaluate the view from seats in scenes, says Marilyn McDonald, StubHub's ranking executive of item, structure, and specialized programs, who tried the component for the Super Bowl in February.

McDonald says StubHub has moved to an item-arranged working model for conveying IT services, predicated on configuration thinking methods of reasoning. "It's tied in with ingraining possession to little, responsible groups," McDonald says. Key to this philosophical move? Guaranteeing that workers have a sense of security enough to come up short, learn, and continue attempting. "Not having the option to come up short is such a heavyweight," she includes.

Cerner

Digital change sometimes requires an ability upgrade or, if nothing else, a strong refresh.

Health-care software giant Cerner is reskilling 10,000 or more workers, including programming engineers familiar with C#, Java RCP, and other legacy programming languages, to figure out how to compose applications for HTML5 and other present-day dialects, says Eric Geis, Cerner's VP of protected innovation improvement.

By embracing a continuous learning society, Cerner is showing a willingness to change with the occasions, Geis says. Cerner has adopted agile, DevOps, and configuration thinking to support Cerner's emergency clinic and clinician clients improve understanding results, he includes. "Greater associations see [the changes] yet are frequently stuck, attempting to break the concrete from their feet and escape from it," Geis says. Cerner is utilizing cutting-edge instructive substance from Pluralsight[xxiv] to prepare existing workers and on-board new ability with educational programs. Cybersecurity is among the different educational plans Cerner has built up utilizing Pluralsight.

"It's certainly assisted with ability maintenance, especially for a current workforce that has been doing the same thing for 10 to 15 years," Geis says. "Offering individuals a constant learning device, give them inspiration and alternatives to prove themselves in the tech space."

Nissan

Nissan is rolling out significant improvements under CIO Tony Thomas, who joined the organization a year ago from GE, where he was filling in as CIO of GE Global. Among Thomas's quick successes was a transition to a digital workplace tied down with Microsoft Office 365 programming, the first of numerous means to streamline and bind together siloed specialty units.

His group is additionally "mobile-enabling" representatives so they can get to corporate applications, for example, Outlook, Skype, and Workday, from their cell phones and tablets. Also on tap are refinements to Nissan's ERP frameworks that will assist data in flowing freely but safely between frameworks to empower business experiences, he says.

Thomas is also assembling more programming in-house, turning around the automaker's longstanding act of redistributing innovation improvement. Building restrictive digital services requires ability, which is the reason Thomas has opened a digital center point in India, which will staff 500 software engineers.

Staff in these center points will take a shot at chatbots, mechanical procedure automation, machine learning, huge information investigation, and different innovations that improve the work understanding for Nissan's 240,000 representatives while additionally quickening the organization's vision of self-ruling vehicles. Chatbots, for example, could make it simpler for clients to discover data about, or even buy, the organization's vehicles, he says, while RPA will robotize errands in Nissan's money and HR tasks. "It's about speed, transparency, and simplicity," Thomas says.

Connex Credit Union

Connex Credit Union CEO Frank Mancini charmed CIO Dennis Klemenz away from Sikorsky Aircraft in 2015 to shepherd another information-based procedure to more readily serve the organization's clients.

From that point forward, Klemenz has divided IT into three units: center handling, which fills in as the bank's brain to facilitate financial transactions; framework, which incorporates a relocation to a private cloud utilizing Nutanix hyper-converged foundation; and investigation and innovation. This keeps chipping away at better sorting out the bank's information and has assembled a Mint-like money-related planning apparatus to assist customers with bettering deal with their wealth health.

Klemenz has also turned out interactive teller machines (ITM) at 12 branches to empower drive-up clients to lead a variety of financial transactions, from pulling out cash to opening accounts from a touchscreen. In August, Connex is opening a mixture branch in Monroe, Connecticut, that uses the two tellers and ITMs, Klemenz says. "The half and half approach isn't a methodology seen much in banking, yet we accept that having tellers and video tellers is the best combo of innovation and hands-on service."

Armstrong World Industries

At the point when CIO Dawn Kirchner-King joined Armstrong World Industries in 2015, IT was a "dark opening cost focus," in which business pioneers didn't have the foggiest idea what they were getting for their cash, Kirchner-King tells CIO.com.

Kirchner-King immediately embraced lean and agile principles upheld by assembling groups at the 150-year-old organization. She gathered daily stand-up gatherings with IT staff and business process pioneers. The groups had a "desire to move quickly we had not had previously," and transparency for the business, who could perceive how their cash was being spent, she says.

"With this transparency came a degree of trust in what we're doing," Kirchner-King says. Concerning the specialized projects, Kirchner-King redesigned ERP money-related applications to the most recent form of SAP, improved and stretched out a Salesforce.com CRM suite to Asia and Europe, and moved to travel the board to Concur. Clients will also take note of another site. "Agile carried speed and earnestness to those projects," says Kirchner-King, who re-apportioned reserve funds to cybersecurity and other basic projects. IT is presently investigating quality issues with its assembling forms, which creates 5,000 information focuses on details, for example, ceiling tile quality and thickness.

Putnam Investments

When Putnam Investments CEO Bob Reynolds approached CIO Sumedh Mehta for an innovation intended to help improve the association's presentation, Mehta urged his colleagues to request arrangements they need, for example, instruments to produce budgetary bits of knowledge for Putnam's money-related consultants. Mehta included Facebook-like joint effort instruments to encourage correspondence among IT and the business, just as Google-like enterprise search abilities and different devices to more readily automate a work process.

Today Mehta is resigning inheritance frameworks, moving applications to the cloud, and putting resources into the examination. Putnam has additionally settled an information science focus of greatness to investigate AI's capacity to produce business bits of knowledge for and about customers. Supporting these moves is a more extensive move toward coordinated wherein IT and business assemble programming in fourteen-day cycles. Mehta says the endeavors have stimulated interest from colleagues ready to grasp better approaches for working. "By making this degree of progress, we had a more grounded engagement with our business people since they were eager to perceive what we took a shot at the prior night," Mehta tells CIO.com. "Organizations that grasp that change will turn into the digital organizations of things to come."

Sprint

Under tension from huge adversaries Verizon and AT&T, and in merger chats with T-Mobile, Sprint is reinvesting in innovation following quite a while of critical cost decrease, says CIO Scott Rice, who is driving the charge. The center is, to a great extent, around breaking down information to improve the client experience.

Sprint is utilizing Elastic Stack open-source programming to beat through 50TB of information created by logs, databases, messages, and different sources to check the presentation of Sprint.com. That information causes IT to figure out where glitches are hindering Sprint's capacity to facilitate transactions, extending from fundamental perusing to telephone purchases, to upgrades buyers are attempting to finish on the web. Investigating bugs and different postpones enables Sprint to decide when and why a client is abandoning an exchange. Beforehand, every application group checked its product execution, making enormous information storehouses that couldn't be utilized to reinforce execution, Rice says. "It's an upgraded [customer] journey dependent on information."

Sprint has additionally made a Hadoop-based information lake to examine client information, with an end goal to improve item proposals to buyers. For instance, a 10-year client of Android telephones will get Android telephone offers. "It's tied in with building a broadness of data about you and your association with us," Rice says. Run's change is proceeding over all parts of the business, and the "IT association is directly in the center of each change project," Rice says, including that he is moving the majority of the association to lithe advancement led in little, self-guided groups to improve software delivery.

You probably won't relate the expression "digital transformation" with a region called Town of Cary, North Carolina. CIO Nicole Raimundo is attempting to make a cut of Silicon Valley in the south. She's wiping out more than 100 heritage applications, including work requests, grants, and onboarding, for Salesforce.com. "I set out on a staged methodology that would empower us to get speedy successes," Raimundo tells CIO.com. The stage, which incorporates field service, IT service management, the board, promoting, and coordinated collaboration tools, is planned to help Raimundo get a 360-degree perspective on Cary's residents, including utility payments, parks, and entertainment class registration and other details.

Raimundo and her staff of 30 also assembled an "ability," basically an application for Amazon Echo that will enable residents to open up work orders and different instruments without utilizing the telephone. Perceiving that individuals progressively wish to encourage exchanges through informing tools, she is additionally investigating the utilization of chatbots to empower residents to start forms with town offices through their telephones. "We will likely meet our residents where they are," she says. Also in progress: Internet of Things, including keen lighting, brilliant stopping, and shrewd reusing on the town's city grounds, which she says fills in as a kind of development lab for rising digital instruments.

As a feature of this enormous culture move, Raimundo has also made open workspaces and has utilized agile and configuration thinking procedures to propel the least reasonable items. The Town of Cary has additionally facilitated hackathons in a perfect world to bait ability from the neighborhood Research Triangle Park, which includes Red Hat, Cisco Systems, IBM, Microsoft, and other top tech vendors. "Those are drivers to bring in the talent we want," she says.

Works Cited

[i] https://www.merriam-webster.com/dictionary/Internet%20of%20Things

[ii] https://innolytics-innovation.com/

[iii] https://www.uber.com

[iv] https://www.airbnb.com

[v] https://www.paytrust.com

[vi] https://www.mycheckfree.com

[vii] https://money.yodlee.com/pfm3/home

[viii] https://www.dwolla.com

[ix] https://www.payoneer.com

[x] https://squareup.com/us/en

[xi] https://quickbooks.intuit.com/payments/mobile/

[xii] https://www.axosbank.com/

[xiii] https://www.bankrate.com/

[xiv] https://www.Books.com

[xv] https://www.osCommerce.com

[xvi] https://www.Magento.com

[xvii] https://www.zen-cart.com/

[xviii] https://www.VirtueMart.net

[xix] https://www.PrestaShop.com

[xx] https://www.ehorus.com

[xxi] https://www.cisco.com/c/en/us/products/security/talos.html

[xxii] https://www.weightwatchers.com/us/how-it-works/Wellow

[xxiii] https://docs.opsgenie.com/docs

[xxiv] https://www.pluralsight.com

References

(Author), Sven. 2020. "GRIN - The Impact Of Digital Life On Society". *Grin.Com.* https://www.grin.com/document/453828.

"5 Reasons To Do Your Banking Online". 2020. *The Balance.* https://www.thebalance.com/three-advantages-of-online-banking-2385804.

"7 Examples Of How Digital Transformation Impacted Business Performance". 2020. *Forbes.Com.* https://www.forbes.com/sites/blakemorgan/2019/07/21/7-examples-of-how-digital-transformation-impacted-business-performance/#6a6f03f251bb.

"7 Examples Of How Digital Transformation Impacted Business Performance". 2020. *Forbes.Com.* https://www.forbes.com/sites/blakemorgan/2019/07/21/7-examples-of-how-digital-transformation-impacted-business-performance/#42207c4b51bb.

"7 Reasons Why You Need To Start Business Digitization Right Now | Rabit Software Engineering". 2020. *Rabit Software Engineering.* https://www.rabitse.com/blog/7-reasons-behind-business-digitization/.

"9 Ways Digital Has Changed Business Forever". 2020. *Digital*

Marketing Institute. https://digitalmarketinginstitute.com/blog/9-ways-digital-has-changed-business-forever.

"9 Ways Digital Has Changed Business Forever". 2020. *Digital Marketing Institute*. https://digitalmarketinginstitute.com/blog/9-ways-digital-has-changed-business-forever.

"9 Ways Digital Has Changed Business Forever". 2020. *Digital Marketing Institute*. https://digitalmarketinginstitute.com/blog/9-ways-digital-has-changed-business-forever.

Boulton, Clint. 2020. "Digital Transformation Examples: An Inside Look At 6 Success Stories". *CIO*. https://www.cio.com/article/3149977/digital-transformation-examples.html?nsdr=true&page=2.

"Cisco Talos - Threat Intelligence Research Team". 2020. *Cisco*. https://www.cisco.com/c/en/us/products/security/talos.html.

"Definition Of INTERNET OF THINGS". 2020. *Merriam-Webster.Com*. https://www.merriam-webster.com/dictionary/Internet%20of%20Things.

"Digitalization Of Life — How Technology Redefine The Self In The Global Context - EASST". 2020. *EASST*. https://easst.net/article/digitalization-of-life-how-technology-redefine-the-self-in-the-global-context/.

Gebski, Todd. 2020. "How Does Technology Impact Your Daily Life?". *Motus | Mobile Workforce Solutions*. https://www.motus.com/how-does-technology-impact-your-daily-life/.

Gebski, Todd. 2020. "How Does Technology Impact Your Daily Life?". *Motus | Mobile Workforce Solutions*. https://www.motus.com/how-does-technology-impact-your-daily-life/.

"How Digital Transformation Impacts Companies - Innovation & Tech Blog". 2020. *ZIGURAT Innovation School - Transform The Way You Do Business!*. https://www.e-zigurat.com/innovation-school/blog/how-digital-transformation-impacts-companies/.

"How Is A List Of Ways To Organize Your Bill-Paying Process". 2020. *The Balance*. https://www.thebalance.com/organize-your-bill-paying-process-3544879.

"How To Pay Your Bills Online". 2020. *The Balance*. https://www.thebalance.com/how-to-pay-your-bills-online-2385977.

"If Our Future Is Digital, How Will It Change The World?". 2020. *WIRED*. https://www.wired.com/insights/2014/04/future-digital-will-change-world/.

Kurzawska, Kate. 2020. "5 Ways In Which Digitization Is Changing Business World - Timecamp". *Timecamp*. https://www.timecamp.com/blog/2018/02/5-ways-digitization-is-changing-business-world/.

"Manage Your Bills Better With Quicken Bill Pay". 2020. *The Balance*. https://www.thebalance.com/pay-online-or-through-quicken-1293897.

Meyer, Dr. 2020. "What Is Digitalization | Innolytics Innovation". *Innolytics Innovation*. https://innolytics-innovation.com/what-is-digitalization/.

"Online Bill Paying Saves Time And Eliminates Paper". 2020. *The Balance*. https://www.thebalance.com/best-online-bill-paying-software-and-services-1293908.

"The 8 Best Online Banks Of 2020". 2020. *The Balance*. https://www.thebalance.com/best-online-banks-4165693.

Tiersky, Howard. 2020. "5 Top Challenges To Digital Transformation In The Enterprise". *CIO*. https://www.cio.com/article/3179607/5-top-challenges-to-digital-transformation-in-the-enterprise.html.

Toren, Adam. 2020. "The 15 Most Popular Online Payment Solutions". *Entrepreneur*. https://www.entrepreneur.com/article/286006.

"Understanding Technology And Its Influence On Human Behavior | Cleverism". 2020. *Cleverism*. https://www.cleverism.com/understanding-technology-and-its-influence-on-human-behavior/.

"Wellow - Your Virtual Wellness Assistant". 2020. *Weightwatchers.Com*. https://www.weightwatchers.com/us/how-it-works/Wellow.

INDEX

Chapter 1 **1**

The Definition of Digital Transformation **1**

    Digitization is the move from analog to digital 2

    Definition of Digitalization 2

    Digitalization is using digital data to simplify how you work 3

    Fields of Digitalization 3

    Digitalization decides the eventual fate of the economy and society 4

    Digitalization changes economy and society 4

    Digitalization and Enterprises 5

    Digital Transformation adds value to customer interaction 7

    Adapt your Business to Leverage Digital Transformation 8

Chapter 2 **11**

Digitization is Changing the Business World **11**

    Artificial Intelligence (AI) 11

    Flexible Work 12

    Innovation 12

    New Business Models 12

    Communication 12

    7 Examples of How Digital Transformation Impacts Business Performance 13

    8 Years at Target 15

    7 Years at Hasbro 16

    2 Years at Home Depot 17

    5 Years at Microsoft 19

    2 Years at Nike 20

3 Years at Honeywell 21

1) Instant Communication 22

2) Content Overload 23

3) Droves of Data 24

4) Demands Transparency 24

5) Fosters Intimacy 25

6) A New Breed of Influencers 26

7) Playing Catch-Up 26

8) Encourage Innovation 27

9) Made Brands More Human 28

Chapter 3 **29**

How Digitalization Impacts Your Daily Life **29**

Our Digitized Professional Lives 29

Technology Gets Personal 30

A New Generation of Digital Natives 30

The Bottom Line 31

Sharing and the New Media 31

You've Got Mail 32

Social Networks 32

Beyond the Bank 32

The Sharing Economy 33

Education 33

New frontiers of health: mHealth and self-administration of sickness 33

Emotional Quantification: happiness as a measure of progress 34

Digital Subjects in Online Spaces 35

Powerful Problems Drive Powerful Dreams 36

Will a New Digital Window Display a New Future? 36

Turn On a You-Centered Digital World 37

Chapter 4 ***40***

*How to Pay Your Bills Online **40***

    Separate Your Bills into Three Piles 40

    Set Up Automatic Drafts 40

    Utilize Your Bank's Payment Service 41

    Decide the Bills You Will Pay Online Each Month 41

    Plan for Your Annual Bills 41

    Tips: 42

    The Most Effective Method to Organize Your Bill-Paying Process 42

    Create a Bill-Paying Station 43

    Organize Your Paper Bills 43

    Organize Your Electronic Bills and Statements 44

    Timetable: a Weekly Time to Pay Your Bills 44

    Pay Your Bills 45

    File the Paper Copies of Your Bill 45

    How to Manage Your Bills Better With Quicken Bill Pay 45

    Advantages of Using Quicken Bill Pay 46

    Utilizing the Bill Pay Service 46

    Setting Up Quicken Bill Pay 46

    Adding Your List of Payees 47

    Best Online Bill Paying Software and Services 48

    Paytrust 48

    Quicken Bill Pay 48

    MyCheckFree 48

    Yodlee 49

    Mint Bills 49

Banks, Brokerages, Credit Cards, and Online Financial Apps 49

Chapter 5 **51**

Banking Online: Online Payment Systems **51**

   1. Due 51

   2. Stripe 51

   3. Dwolla 52

   4. Apple Pay 52

   5. Payoneer 52

   6. 2Checkout 52

   7. Amazon Payments 53

   8. Square 53

   9. Skrill 53

   10. Venmo 53

   11. Google Wallet 54

   12. WePay 54

   13. Intuit GoPayment 54

   14. Authorize.net 54

   Five Advantages of Online Banking 55

   Take care of Your Bills Online 55

   View your Transactions 56

   Move Money Between Accounts 56

   Mobile Banking 57

   Synchronizing With Your Money Applications 57

   Online-Only Banks 57

   Secure Yourself Online 58

   Online Banking 59

   Online Banking Fraud 59

Online Banking—Bank with Caution 60

Understanding Online Banking 60

Online Banking Services 62

Security 64

Best Overall: Ally Bank 66

Best for Those in Big Cities: Capital One 66

Best for Frequent Travelers: Charles Schwab Bank 67

Best for Budgeting: Simple 67

Best Old-School Option: Axos Bank 68

Best for Rewards Checking: Discover Bank 68

Best for College Students: Chime 69

Best for High Balance Checking Accounts: TIAA Bank 69

1) Account Management 70

2) Deposits and Payments 70

3) Debit Card 70

4) E-statement 71

How to Set Up Online Banking 71

Utilizing Card Readers 72

How To Use Online Banking 72

1. Comfort 73

2. Direct Control Over Your Transactions 74

3. Access to Everything All in One Place 74

4. Lower Banking Fees and Higher Interest Rates 75

5. Paperless Statements 75

6. Automated Account Alerts 75

7. Advanced Security 76

Chapter 6 *78*

Shopping Online 78

    History 78

    Beginnings 78

    Growth 78

    Clients 79

    Merchants 80

    Logistics 80

    Payment 81

    Item Delivery 82

    Shopping Cart Frameworks 83

    Web Site Design 83

    Online Shopping And Retail Shopping 85

    Shipping 86

    Trends 87

    Concerns 88

    Fraud and Security Concerns 88

    Privacy 89

    The Dos And Don'ts In Online Shopping 90

    DOs: 90

    DON'TS: 91

    Benefits of Shopping Online 91

    Disadvantages of Online Shopping 93

Chapter 7 96

Digital Economy 96

    Digital Economy vs. Internet Economy 96

    Significance of the Digital Economy 97

    Digital Technologies 97

Entrepreneurs in the Digital Economy 97

Digital Transformation Examples 98

Rushes of Interruption 98

The Future of the Digital Economy 99

How Should We Measure the Digital Economy? 99

What GDP Doesn't Measure 100

(1) Taxation 102

(2) E-payments, Fin-tech, and Other Mechanical Guidelines 103

(3) AI 104

(4) Information Disclosure of Firms and Measurements 104

(5) Due Procedure in Government Access to Security/Industry Information 104

6. Mechanical Policy and Strategic Trade and Investment Policies 105

7. The Way Ahead 105

The Underrated Boost from the Digital Economy 107

Measure correctly 108

The Missing Link 109

The Next Productivity Boom 110

The Advantages and Difficulties of the Digital Economy for Developing Countries 111

First-order Benefits 111

Second-order benefits 112

Implications 115

Public Value 123

Citizen Security 124

Smart Infrastructure 126

Risks in e-governance Systems 127

Modus Operandi of Attackers 127

    Spoofing 128

    Tampering of E-Governance framework 128

    Repudiation 128

    Exposure of E-Governance Information 129

    Denial of service 129

    Elevation of privilege 129

    Cybercrimes 129

    False or malicious website 129

    Theft of citizens' information from intermediary agents and ISPs 129

    Violation of citizens' privacy through the use of cookies 130

    Spamming and flaming 130

    Citizen impersonation 130

    Ping of Death 130

    Teardrop 130

    Intranet-associated threats 131

Risks associated with stored online E-Governance Information 131

The risk associated with malicious code 131

The Advantages of Electronic-Government 131

The Disadvantages of Electronic-Government 132

What does e-Government Cover? 133

    Interfacing Citizens: e-Citizens and e-Services 135

    Building External Interactions: e-Society 135

Chapter 8 ***137***

Why digitization is important for your business 137

    Industries that have embraced digitization well 138

    Digitization is Significant for Your Business 140

Understanding Digitalization

1. Your industry is open for interruption 140

2. You have to improve ordinary productivity 141

3. You must offer the best client experience 142

4. Utilizing new channels to their maximum capacity 143

5. Think about mobile users 144

6. Your production network 145

7. Use innovations 146

– Digital presence 147

– New contact channels with clients 148

– The client at the core of the universe 148

– Better basic leadership 148

– It improves proficiency and profitability 149

– It encourages innovation 149

– It makes communication and teamwork easier 149

– It improves working conditions 149

   Generation C 152

The world readily available 152

The power of apps 152

Types of applications for businesses 154

1. Loyalty applications 154

2. Office productivity apps 154

3. Mobile CRM and sales support apps 155

4. Business-explicit apps 155

5. Appointment scheduling apps 155

Chapter 9 ***156***

Challenges with Digitization 156

   Challenge 1: Data Management: 156

Challenge 2: Self-Controlling 157

Challenge 3: Agile Control 157

Challenge 4: Efficiency in Controlling 158

Challenge 5: Business Partnering 158

Challenge 6: Analytics 159

Challenge 7: New Skills 160

Challenge 8: Controlling Mind-set 160

The Art of Connecting Everything 161

Standards 161

Big Data 162

Security 162

Skills and Jobs 163

Proof of Value 163

Understanding and Anticipating Impact 163

Why organizations battle to develop digital strategies 164

How CIOs can drive change 165

Chapter 10 ***167***

*Case studies **167***

Digital Transformation Success Stories 167

WW 168

Atlassian 169

StubHub 169

Cerner 170

Nissan 171

Connex Credit Union 172

Armstrong World Industries 172

Putnam Investments 173

Sprint 174

www.ingramcontent.com/pod-product-compliance
Lightning Source LLC
Chambersburg PA
CBHW052351220526
45465CB00003BA/1058